First Published 2009 by Templar Poetry
Templar Poetry in an imprint of Delamide & Bell
Fenelon House
Kingsbridge Terrace
58 Dale Road,
Matlock,
Derbyshire
DE4 3NB

www.templarpoetry.co.uk

ISBN 978-1-906285-85-2

Typeset by Pliny
Graphics by Paloma Violet
Printed and bound in India

Iota

Iota 85

Contacting Iota

Website: www.iotamagazine.co.uk
Editor: editor@iotamagzine.co.uk
Features: features@iotamagzine.co.uk
Listings: listings@iotamagazine.co.uk
Subscriptions: subs@iotamagazine.co.uk
Distribution & Sales please refer to the website
Please send correspondence & Submissions to:

Iota
PO Box 7721
Matlock
DE4 9DD

Design & Layout:
Raphael Tassini & Paloma Violet
Printed & Bound in India

Cover Image: Cappucino in the Ai Do Draghi, Veneto

Iota
ISSN 0266-2922
ISBN 978-1-906285-85-2

www.iotamagazine.co.uk
£6.50 $11.50 €8.00

Contents

Editorial

I am happy to report that the initial feedback on issue 83/84 has been everything we'd hoped. Almost immediately there were letters and blog posts complimenting both the external beauty and the quality of the contents. We hope that enthusiasm continues and that this issue pleases its readers as much as the previous one.

The two issues are quite different in feel, the last issue contained a high proportion of work from North America, this issue is much more UK and Irish centred. It is none the worse for that. It may be that some in the UK were waiting to see what happened with the change of editorship before submitting, which lead to a bulge in UK work submitted in the months we were reading for this issue. Perhaps after the North American feel to the last issue, the editors unconsciously wanted something with a more homely flavour. Whatever processes resulted in this selection, we are very happy with it and we hope that you will enjoy it.

I am delighted to see the appointment of Carol Ann Duffy as Poet Laureate. I think that it will be a good appointment for poetry for several reasons: as the first woman appointed to the post, she has finally broken a barrier which has previously stopped excellent female poets, Elizabeth Barret Browning, Christina Rossetti among them, from taking the most prestigious honour that British poetry has to offer. Though I have to say that it makes me sad to see that in 2009 this is still an issue.

Secondly, she seems to be a generous soul who is genuinely interested in the promotion of, and widening the audience for, poetry. So much so that she has elected to give her yearly stipend for the Laureateship back to poetry. I applaud her for that. Though I'm not sure another collection prize is the way to go. We already have several big money collection prizes and I'm not sure another would add much. What I'd like to see is a prize for 'widening participation in poetry'. That prize might go to a publisher, an event organiser, a poet, or anyone who comes up with a way to significantly increase the participation of the general public in poetry. Rewarding that might really do some good for all poetry and all poets.

Thirdly, I think that she will make an excellent ambassador for poetry. Her work is on most of the school syllabi. A whole generation are already familiar with at least some of her work, which is both good and accessible. Many others will have been aware of her work through the removal of 'Education for Leisure' and the controversy of the subject matter. That means a significant proportion of the population will know her as a poet. I have no doubt that many will go back to read her work now, if only out of idle curiosity. One would hope that many of those who do, will find poetry has something to offer them.

I am aware that many poets will not agree with my logic in this, there are poets who will argue that they don't want a mass audience for their work. I see their point, they write, they would argue, for a select few who have the necessary background reading and awareness of poetic and theoretical concepts to appreciate their work. Okay, but if we can re-engage the general public with the best accessible poetry, perhaps they will go on to acquire the breadth of reference to read this more experimental work with the sophistication the poets concerned demand of their readers. This is not about making a case for 'Poetry Lite'. It's about an endeavour to allow the public to re-engage with the whole spectrum of poetry out there: performance based work, accessible, mainstream, or experimental (insert your own labels as you wish). The idea is that if someone comes to poetry through performance poetry or through accessible work, they just might be persuaded to try more experimental work later on. They might discover that their 'taste' was broader than they first thought. Which brings me back to the idea for the prize. If we had a major prize that rewarded initiatives that widened participation in poetry, it would inevitably lead to more creativity and activity in that direction.

It is with deep regret that the Editorial Board of Iota note the death of U.A. Fanthorpe, one of the finest contemporary English poets, who was an Honorary Doctor and Fellow of the University of Gloucestershire. We extend our sympathies to her partner R.V. Bailey on her loss. She will be greatly missed, but her work will continue to be read. We would like to dedicate this issue to her.

Nigel McLoughlin
Editor
May 2009

Poetry

Howard Wright

Centrum

Lakes wear synthetic fleece; villages sink like coins
into upholstery. Mountains buckle under the strain.
I skirt the pleated hemline of the smooth stewardess
who sets me down in central Europe, its batik fields,
slide rules and bearded masters of game theory.

My bilingual change speaks volumes. I buy prints
of the Forgotten District where a leadership is buried;
browse a library of mourning stone, its chiselled
screams like recordings of death's awkward rituals,
and through needle rain circle the Empty Quarter

drawn by whispers to a solemn river stitched with
bridges, spokes from the ur-centre – hub and spindle –
suspended from squadrons of angels folded like sick
pigeons bloated with darkness, right wing government,
and a culture that replaces feathers with industrial ash.

Contraband

smugglers buy the road
a rainbow on fire
above smoke on the hill
of headstones
slouching
towards the exit

blue bags of cans
in ditch and trees
the pink condom
a flattened foreskin
the barrack-buster
homemade cooked up

to go with the shell cases
and pipebombs
plastic cows poured
from a box and rattled
worshipful cows
wallowing centre circle

a puddle of sky
the camouflaged kids
inside a winter hedge
fencing two-handed
with light sabres
minus batteries

Vertigo

i

Kindred gorse burnt in the last week
by woodkerne makes the air hurt and close
with heat and ash; the rose-bay on a broad front
like an army stubborn in advance,
the undergrowth embers of blackened bones,

hindquarters, forelegs of errant cavalry
outflanked on the shank of the mountain,
banners of smoke, streaming these long days,
both a clearance and a warning...

ii

Where the wolf stood, now we stand
with everything before us except a future.

The angled, fractured city is a clinking blanket
of crockery bundled up, awkwardly held,
when the meal is over and the talk run out.

iii

We think there are places we know:
bridges with rivers up to their armpits;
the factories, schools, wards in their green pockets,
their bright flat swards like spaces tacked on,
because it isn't lives we think of; anything but.

iv

We just make the summit. Others have walked here
so long ago they have fallen into history.
None among us promises to come back.

From Cornmarket

i

High Street glows through the haze,
the city printing itself on the smoke.
Hold it up for flaws. It soaks in the same
milky light as an unbreakable twenty.
Those entries and arcades, *The Twilight Zone*
where you lose an arm and a leg
to three-eyed thugs; the 'Imbibing Emporium'
so grandly stated the original frontage
brims like a glass of stout.

ii

Swirls of starlings, a banner made
from collective instinct. Short-term memory
as a long-term goal. Gulls attack the beerguts
of taxi-touts, and politicians run about
like ducks in thunder, policies
as radical as a hole in the ground.
The culture of drink narrows
pavements and spills untamed
women into the gutter.

iii

Let shadows flock to Cavehill
and dragonflies skim Divis. Up there,
history thickens. Down here,
the unfurnished deserts are built
as redoubts against Whitewell,
Whiterock, Whiteabbey,
their petticoat outskirts slipping over
stubble fields like waves over sand
continually destroying themselves.

The Ocean

I will bring you to the ocean,
the beginning of a memory
like the beginning of a poem,
both now in the making,
your pale coat flapping
and hands full of stuff
from the world's edge
and the water at your heels,
your smile filling the sky...

I will bring you to the ocean
because you must show me
what we are there for,
the heart of a memory
or a poem, or the horror
of not being there at all,
only me dreaming as you
empty your hands of the flotsom
until there is nothing left.

Howard Wright lectures in Fine and Applied Arts at the University of Ulster, Belfast. Recent poems have appeared in *Poetry Ireland* and *Cyphers*. His first collection, *King of Country,* is in preparation at Blackstaff Press

Intimated

One morning when the world had not yet crossed my ego,
I and he went for a drive, the two of us who were not a pair,
leaving the others to sleep.
I can't remember where we went.
It was early spring, tarmac-sleet dark;
nothing stirred on the long wept roads
save the usual patrol dogs padding the oily mist.
I can't tell you the words. Our voices
spoke and wheeled, spinning tales,
scaling far where the camber rose and fell.
It was Sunday, not our country or our car,
and the unproven border fleshed red and green.

The Beach Hawker

He rarely eats
the fruit he sells,
preferring instead the skin.
The shiny wax that covets the apple
the singular greens of shapely pears,
and how bananas spoon each other
to brown the peel, freckle.

In youth a lover took him in
and made him gifts
of fat black grapes and sugary limes,
raised on fine white tissue.
And where she touched
left stains of light, the like of which
he could not bear; for love could not remove.

So that now,
when comparing peach with apricot
(as he often does on his rounds) -
he nearly always
plumps on the side of the latter.
Regards the drying fibres sweetly
approves in time their soft defeat.

The hawker sits
on his splintered crate, to eye
the seedling ships. The beach is empty
in noonday sun and familiar trickles
of icy fruit seep their way down peeling thighs.
He weights his feet in snow, in sand,
bathes thinning flesh, reflects.

Jane Speare lives in Hackney, East London, and works in teacher education. She attends poetry classes at Morley College.

When my father made toy trains

When my father made toy trains
the house was alive with engines and carriages,
red, blue, yellow, green.

All the kids in the alley drilled wheels
in a shower of gold. We were going places
at sixpence an hour,

perhaps to a boarding-house by the sea
although my mother refused to cook or make beds.
It's all right for you just talking to people.

Next a Chinaman
ran down our road pulling a rickshaw.
Cheaper in Woolworths with a cactus inside

and lastly a telephone table, classy
with flecked oak and glass reflecting his dreams.
Underneath the directories packed with his customers.

Monday morning again, he'd say,
snapping the bike clips round his ankles
like manacles.

My mother's kitchen

My mother's kitchen is empty now.
It has all been cleared -
the dead geraniums, the cooker
she could no longer use,
the green cupboards my father
fitted in the 1950's, the bowls,
the china with the leaping stag,
the potatoes bubbling round the joint,
the recipes on faded paper.

She's wheeled up to the table now
remembering sometimes in a slide of mind
that saucepan, those dents,
a tea-towel with heraldic arms,
the castles she visited in Spain.

John Daniel is published in a wide variety of magazines. A Winner of the Exeter prize and commended in last year's National, his poems have also appeared in anthologies - *23 British Poets* (Swallow) and *Faber Introduction series*. A volume, *Missing the Boat*, was published last year by Etruscan Books.

Silk Road Dreams
(after Colin Thubron)

An old woman sleeps by a holy spring.
She has a thirst dreams slake.
Her head rests on an alder root,
her bunched form swaddled in skirts
and the tattered coat she married in once.

Brides mount the steps,
bouquets and glittering brooches,
a fuss of relatives. They stand
beneath the President, his stern
stone look, his birdlime epaulettes.

Behind them come unsmiling grooms,
like plainclothes police in regulation suits.
She looks for his face among them
but he's gone, dissolved
before she can make out if it's him.

Now she's crossing a desert. A suit of armour
sprawls before her. She lifts the vizor.
A face that could be his or could be
her brother's stares through centuries
and says: I'm hurt. Don't let me die.

She's climbing steps again, worn
hexagonal stones through willow
and swallowsong. The buddha of the future
sits fat with history like an outsized doll
squeezed stuck in a gateway.

A monk approaches, fumbling a tin bowl.
She fishes out her housekey, drops it in.
He signs for her to follow. At the river
wading women link arms in the moonlight
feeling for jade with their toes.

Notes towards charmed lives

for the beautiful
the modesty of a hellebore

for the thoughtful
a new idea oxidising in the air

for the deaf
the wing beat of a moth trapped in a cello

for the shy
the close attention of shadow

for the homeless
no false haven, no landlord's ransom

for the widower
the bridal white of crab-apple blossom

for the ambitious
a sneak preview of posterity

for the lost
a story to navigate by

for the introspective
a mirror smashed by fireworks

for the not yet departed
the sound of snow covering tracks

Mike Barlow won the National Poetry Competition in 2006. He has two collections, *Living on the Difference* (Smiths Doorstop) and *Another Place* (Salt). His pamphlet, *Amicable Numbers*, was a winner in the 2008 Templar Competition and a Poetry Book Society Pamphlet Choice.

Facing 50 with a Line by Robert Hayden

There is so much that clings to us —
not just cat fur and grass

seed, but also chocolate

creams and the white beach
of childhood, an extended sash of blue.

*

Not just sadness and solace,

but what the body
reveals after waking,

the open heart and a watery

sense of who we are, the life we attempt to choose.

*

What clings to us (train trips, questions)
fall forward to all

the future will randomly

reduce to an email, an hour,
a knot of pleasure — nearly pursued.

*

The seasons clock on

redecorating the light we crave
like a dim-sum tray —

rich, sensual, and brand new

to each other —

      *

as Shakespearean fools, as Pomeranians,

a bright pair of trusted boots.

Letter to the End of the Year

Lately, I am capable of small things.

Peeling an orange.
Drawing a bath.
Throwing the cat's tinsel ball.

Believe me, this is not unhappiness.

Only one question –
why this layering on of abeyance?

Though it is winter inside of me –

there is also spring and fall.

Yellow tulips in need of planting
root in a basket by the door.

Tonight, mortality seems cloistered in a pinecone

close-windowed, remote.

What was the peak moment
of your happiness?

And how did you know?

For weeks, it's been oatmeal,
the Internet, an Irish shawl.

I realize, I am growing older
and stranger.

Please, don't misunderstand.

I am still impatient
still waiting for symbiant and swoon
      the litter of blue-gold –

      a one-time constellation:

Now, before you go.

History of a Kiss

And, if they are lovers —
is this the first kiss

or their mother's final
sparkling sorrow?

The children with their hats
cast down

cannot recall
the man's calm eyes, his animal coat

but all their lives
the taint of his cologne

cinnamon and thyme —
will keep them

seeking love's illusions
committing all its crimes.

Susan Rich has received awards from the Academy of American Poets and PEN USA. She is the author of *Cures Include Travel* and *The Cartographer's Tongue*. Recent poems will appear in *The Antioch Review, Harvard Review,* and *Poetry International*. Her collection, *The Alchemist's Kitchen*, will be published next year.

Urban Myths

Brown belts and black belts
look out from the judo window,
swings run the gauntlet of gravity,
little kids move on to the Flying Fox.

Bats eavesdrop upside-down from telegraph wires,
owls send each other hoot-mails.
And the Pied Piper of Redland Green
puts on his storytelling cap

and tells of the tortoise family who set off
on a picnic of pineapple, papaya and mango.
Such a Galapagos sense of perfection,
three years to find a grassy green glade,

two years while baby tortoise is sent off
to find a tin-opener. Famished while waiting
father tortoise grabs a guilty sandwich.
'I knew you'd start without me.'

Then the children who listen lose patience,
overtaken by sleep like the hare in the fable.
And the lights go out
on their little leveret lives.

Jardin De Luxembourg

On a chicken-run of rough terrain,
jackets, granddad cardigans rigged up
on coat-hangers on a metal frame.

A woman throws the *cochonnet*.
An arthritic man picks up his boule
with a magnet on a string and hurls.

Another with a tremor
lobs with a backward flip and takes
his opponent's out on the full volley.

Athletes of the third age
hiding their rage
under the paulownia trees.

From a Different Palette

They want a Charley's Aunt of a painting
that runs and still goes on running

where sheep bivouac in the gorse
and sing round the campfire at night

where cattle tramp their hooves on the common
and cowpats buzz with sultana-brown horse-flies

where bees pinball through vetch,
speedwell and celandine

where colours go quiet in the coulisses

They want California poppies
that wear phallic gnome's caps before they unbud

They want red and white geraniums
that turn blowsy as old ladies' bathing caps

They want a painting that changes its linen every day

Forget my something-else of a painting
where I dip my brush in a cowpat and just paint.

Pedant in the Kitchen

"Psychology is in its infancy as a science"

Tall coffee pot and milk jug
with a wicked sense of spillage.
The day's folded *Times* to be cut open
with a paper knife.
Tiny marmalade spoon and butter-knife
with Cutler's name in cursive script.

An unseen ten commandments:
Plate, cup and saucer
in matching family livery.
A boiled egg, oval,
to be taken as it is.
No toast seeds in the butter.

No stray peels of marmalade.
Triangles of toast
from a mathematics text-book
on a rectangular silver rack.
They breathe on eggshells,
never break the bread of friendship

and rarely break the silence.

Michael Henry studied Modern Languages. He lives in Cheltenham and has published five collections, four with Enitharmon Press, the latest, *After the Dancing Dogs*, came out in 2008.

Train from Penn Station

Leaving Manhattan there are station stops with names
I can't pronounce, and ones with hints of fantasy.
Mineola – a breakfast cereal bar. Syosset –
a soft, milk pudding; maybe served with pears.
Hicksville – a place I'd thought unreal: a sitcom
movie-town out in the sticks; sweet serenity
in the U, S of A. Then, Cold Spring Harbor –
a contradiction in my head: freshwater springs
and ocean harbours. Fresh and salt together,
an oxymoron. But sure enough, when my host
takes me for a drive across Long Island the water
pools right in and out, tracing such loops
of wonder. The lines that divide us are so thin.
I see an osprey perched on a post, waiting to fish.

Cross-section

Harlem River: smell of salt-fish, stench of garbage. A new
road is being built, and workers have cut through a knoll
to level in 9th Avenue. William L. Carver is looking at the raw side
of earth when he sees bones. Using his cane he pokes away

at the shell-like surround; deduces the bones belong to a dog.
Later he finds other dog skeletons. He thinks they've been buried
like rotten meat; that the natives used to eat their dogs then
throw out the bones. William and his friend Reginald Pelham Bolton

are trained engineers, part-time archeologists. It is 1895.
These gentlemen dig (weather permitting) in white shirt, coat and tie.
They are dedicated, but cannot imagine the past with empathy.
All told, eleven dogs are uncovered. The men never think that these

are proper burials, yet the dogs were not thrown aside like rubbish;
they were laid to sleep like the deceased people of the same
Late Woodland era. Each dog is curled nose to tail in its grave,
then blanketed in oyster shells mixed with fragments of fired clay.

NB the Late Woodland period is between 1000 and 500 years BCE

Cath Nichols' publications are *Tales of Boy Nancy,* a pamphlet (Driftwood Publications 2005) and *My Glamorous Assistant* (Headland Press, 2007).

Derrick Buttress

The Dictator's Apple

A snapshot, 1935

The man with the comic moustache
lies on a bank of grass peeling an apple
with a folding pocket knife.
He clutches the handle of bone,
cuts the peel, a wriggling strip,
as if this trivial act
must be performed to perfection.

He's alone, peeling his apple.
Now he's slicing the pure white fruit.
This slice is the Sudetenland.
He pops it into his mouth. It is sweet.
This slice is Poland, and the next is Russia.
He chews the fruit seriously.

When he has eaten the whole of the apple
he wipes his knife on the grass,
tests the sharpness of the blade
with the ball of his thumb,
stares into the cold blue metal of the sky
as though he's dreaming.

The Drag Act's Story

The flimsy glamour was like an itch
that nothing in my life could sooth.
I drove most nights to beer-soured halls
where the air was a smoke-filled lung
and dust-motes drifted in the spotlight.
I loved it all, lived out my dream.

After the bingo and the M.C.'s smut
I faced the terror of an empty stage,
the old patter unwinding in my head.
I was Fanny *'Still a Virgin'* Snivel,
an old tart in a party frock,
five-inch heels and a beehive wig.

My comic liturgy of bad luck and sex
challenged the tanked up crowd to laugh
at the artful misery they knew so well.
And I reached out to them,
tried to conjure a kind of love between us,
nursing the aching secret of myself as I sang
my walk-off song, the limping schmaltz
of my frail *goodnight, goodnight, god bless!*

Derrick Buttress is widely published in magazines and his poems have been broadcast on Radio. His three collections of poetry are: *Spiking The Boss's Gin* (Mo-Saic, 1998), *Waiting For the Invasion* (Shoestring, 2002) and *My Life As A Minor Character* (Shoestring, 2005).

Poem for a Blind Daughter

(after Kate Clanchy)

We thought you'd like to know:

that the colour of my eyes, which is also yours,
smells of the sea, pungent
with bladder wrack, flecked with an approaching storm,

that your father's hair, which is also yours,
is the sound of a stone lobbed into the deepest well,
splashing, then stilled,

that you're likely to inherit our height,
which tastes of the cool, peat-laden spring
at the furthest reaches of Loch Maree,

that the shade of your skin
is smooth as the finest sand of Ullapool,
kissed repeatedly by a loving tide,

that you live in a tall, white building,
high above the ocean,
where one day, you will own the brightest eye.

Storm in Wirksworth Churchyard

There is something urgent about
        this morning, the white rose bush
ravaged, an old lady
        in her petticoats, feathers, lace
sprawled beneath her.

Blackbirds unsettled, even
        the shaven-headed man with the swallows
on his neck has stayed away.
        Waves break across the tombstones,
a bell warns of worse to come.

There'll be a reckoning. The light
        hardly knows how to settle before it is blown
elsewhere. A plastic noise as the air vent skips
        clean through the window.
In the cellar an uncorking.

Somewhere in the house a door cracks
        its shriek of lightning.
The silver birch goes on fighting
        itself, a small civil war
in the corner of the yard.

A roaring from the yew, a shifting
        of shadows. Leaves come away early,
their fistful of daggers rip
        into the oak of the church door.
A tolling, way way out at sea.

Katrina Naomi's pamphlet *Lunch at the Elephant & Castle* (2008) is published by Templar Poetry. Her first collection, *The Girl with the Cactus Handshake* will be published in autumn 2009 by Templar Poetry.

The Bed Wetter

He sat up
as if brought in from the snow.
Compromised by fog
he stumbled to gather words,
mid-sentence chiffon, lace
ruffling memory.

Sisters
knew his shame;
soupy springs
hot with acids
a smoking dream;
perseverance on his cheek
redder than talk.
Slit-grin pyjamas.

The Date

he split, a mirror,
unbalancing image,
his tingling front

> candle flickering,
> flesh tones

hairs erect themselves
uninterrupted upon
Anthony's back

> cornelian wine,
> crushed berries,
> a jar

closing eyes
half way
he could feel the pressure
of bulges

> music playing
> scumbling conversation,
> pungent garlic air

each time they parted
the moon blinked,
velvet eye

> low viewpoint,
> a tablecloth
> snap – bread

they'd eaten well
exchanging looks
swallowed passion,
red-hot peppers

The Catch And Its Fisherman

Slow into vespers
he paddles in shadows,
dormant piquant air,
doner kebabs,
sea-grey mists, raw umber
whiff, cobbled streets.

Humbling bridge
each rivet a lymphatic glitch.

Piss steaming a curry house
doorway, spiked heels clacking
maw-cry, the same pitch,
curdling stomach.

A photograph,
today's paper —
a killer with slicked-back hair,
rusty nose, a buoy.

A hot chill
fillets his spine,
rat scurry, dead fish,
hulking distance, lights.

Christopher Barnes has written poetry reviews for *Poetry Scotland* and *Jacket Magazine*.

Bastille Day

Humans drink and eat on café patios,
       approximate telepathy on telephones,
       whistle Bach — a remote-controlled toy
       dumptruck revs along the sidewalk
       past a book shop, a jam-and-honey shop,
       a radio station, delivering a parcel to the clinic.

In a parked American sedan, an American citizen
       swallows lithium with mango juice —
       she thumbs a switch on a remote.

Lithium in pure form is a soft,
       white-silver metal, oxidizing
       rapidly in air or water, the lightest
       non-gaseous element, heat of fusion,
       3 kJ/mol.

As the clinic explodes, she's trying to
       remember a man's long name — who
       spearheaded the Manhattan Project?

Rings around the stem
       of a mushroom cloud
       are intermediately wide
       between the rings
       of gods and married men.

The model shows "islands" and/or
       "peninsulas" of populations
       inside "seas" of other populations
       are the likely areas for violence.

Once every generation on Earth: Sun, Earth,
       Jupiter, Saturn in syzygy.

Protecting further violence studies against accusations
     of demonizing certain populations,
     the "islands" model also can be used
     to assay the mindless and objective
     contents of a test tube, for example,
     oil (a little) and water (ample).

Sushi Bar

Precise — these lengths
of snapper flesh,
arranged on a black, square dish —

eight-petaled star.
I am still hungry,
my intestines in good health.

With that rigid-necked grace particular
to dancers, milady
stands, squints

at me, leaves the bar — *no*
shit sister-flower
forgiven, squint white

suns crack, marble
pieces, red veins
in the marbles, piece of eight, white

blood coins on
the eyes, beams kiss
the sea, what are all these kissings worth,

if thou kiss not me?

T. Zachary Cotler's poems can be found in recent issues of *The Wolf, New Review of Literature, Antioch Review, FIELD, Conjunctions.* New poems will be in the upcoming issues of *Post Road* and *Paris Review*.

Your Different Lights

I like you in the half light,
your head tucked under my shelf,
and your eyelashes beating shades
of spiders' legs fallen thick down your face.
By globe-light, as you spin the world with
your finger and tell me rivers
and capital cities, I know your bones
as journeys your cheeks take.

Standing day-lit at the southern window,
a silhouette of man blocking light; your blank mass,
there to be guessed, filled in by squinting.

By 3am car-light, it is you
through the windscreen, stopped bent
to scare a pheasant to the verge
(this sapphire-necked bird paralysed,
baffled by tarmac and you, creeping),
so sweet and sober, tip-toed,
shoo-handed. You both look up.
Caught robbers, struck direct by stars.

Yvonne Eller

Metaphor

Today, I am a pseudo-other.
That is,
I'm not at all sure
that I should even be here.
For example, I missed a phone call
by split-seconds. All the way home I saw
words on backs of vans,
hints in tea-leaves.

Sadly, I gather, I'm cross-living. Perhaps I'm in your shoes.
You could be in mine, or elsewhere; I don't think we can cohabit.

I expect
I zipped across, wrongly, by some
slipstream trick in a bad decision,
inheriting the most proximal future
and bursting out, like new
shoots at a growing point.

Last week, I felt my bones click into place each morning
as audible ticks in boxes to say
I'm charting well according to
the eager workings out of many
winged men by a great unfurled map, whose creased
coordinates include words like 'twenty
-two and a half' and 'conversation
had with mother' or 'endured exhibition
of MDF doors'.

Also, I remember spotting a long unseen friend across
the street, and a quilted old-style handbag
in just the right shade,
when out to buy hubcaps. I recall
feeling at home with the sun drenching
my upturned face, patio peach tea
and a giggly sense that leaving really was
best for all concerned.

This week is different, dire.
Your life pinches my toes. There have been
many mishaps, property papers, out-kiltered hand-signals,
full deaf hours of lost advice,
and birthday cards, belated.

Trying to mix myself
cake-like into a different life cannot be
the sole activity of myself. Logic requires
that we all must switch at once.
(This must cause more panic in the lofty offices
than can be imagined, cuing
hefty paperwork,
clues to trajectories best re-routed, whispers
in the trees, the resurfacing
of long-lost treasures in arrow lines; sweets on the floor.)

Next week when I'm back – if I am – I shall never be
too sure of being
myself,
instead assuming
a good humoured policy of Pascalian wager.

I shall think nothing of wearing odd socks. I shall learn tea-leaf.

Mobile: On deciding to keep it on the seventh day after both you and my mother independently informed me that my main problem is indecision

There are times when I think our parting
would reverse nature.
(Think of Aristophanes'
revolting hermaphrodites, struck down by Zeus,
torn in two to prevent an uprising and left
in halves cursed to seek themselves forever;
There would have been lightning bolts,
a desert and blindness, like Rapunzel's saviour
flailing; damage by thorns.)

I do not call you my other half.
We are more like two fingers, crossed.
In fact, on this wet Wednesday evening, I wonder
if our combined, doubled weight
could limit us when we'd be better off
floating untrained, paying as we go.
Or if love much cares for gravity,
let alone time.

If I am temporarily blinded by the completion
of inclusivity contracts, which bind me
in all terms and conditions, ultimately
to yourself,
forgive me.
I can take you, 2 for 1,
to the giant screen
next Wednesday evening.

Yvonne Eller is a recent graduate of the University of Nottingham in Philosophy and English Studies.

Skye Blues

the constellation of Mallaig
turns on its harbour lights
and sends silver filaments
across the Christmas water
like lost strands of lametta

the Ardvasar Hotel gives up
its obligation to celebrate

brown untidy bungalows
provide a kitch spectacle
of bruised plastic snowmen
and sparkle-eyed reindeer
leaping electric blue icicles

dwarfs climb a snow-ladder
looking whisky malicious
and ready to snatch back
any gift Santa might give

we're a couple of silhouettes
in front of a neon sleigh
warming ourselves on disdain

our New Year was a duty
and we are tired of caring

sorry for our bad temper
and what we failed to do
until the night hushes us
with an abracadabra of stars

Weather Man

his little metallic frame
welcomed raindrops
and sticky dying insects

water looked good on him
lingering the right amount
to accept soft shadows

his law was pointing
to a prevailing emotion
as if he had no dream
or desire for blizzards
across his black brow

his honest edge turned
to the strongest wind -
nothing frightened him
except doldrum skies

in neglected gardens
he offered no resistance
to the change coming

until the wind stole
his immortal soul

Robin Lindsay Wilson, graduated from the Royal Scottish Academy of Music & Drama.
He now works as Head of Acting at Queen Margaret University, Edinburgh. His first
collection is *Ready Made Bouquets* (Cinnamon Press)

The Language of Birds

She is singing French songs
through the bars of the cage

to the lovebird pecking
the cuttlebone, called Peter,

which, in the Bible, means "rock"—
but he is a clockwork of minuscule bones

draped, like a fog, in feathers.
He preens each day before the glass

and plays games he cannot win—
pin the button to the bars,

tap the code on a piece of horn,
the code no-one can decipher,

tear the newspaper with a toothless
beak, wear down the block of salt.

It is only vowels between them now,
pure vowels, and glass-like trills,

sounds reclaimed from the top of the tower
of Babel. He rings his bell, he strums

the bars, uncurls his wings as though
these sounds could somehow give him lift.

To Friends Not Knowing What to Say

to J. V.P.,   B. Jan. 24, 2006   D. Jan. 27, 2006

It is mine
        to bear, this sack
                of dust, broken
rhythms of night's
        covered drum.

The wind has something
                to tell me.
Look how it tugs
        at my sleeve.

In a dream,
        I disown the alphabet,
unsaying each letter
        in a song.

Who can repair
        the questions
to make them hold
        water or bones?

The drum renounces
        its echo.

Bagpipes offer us
        the reed's endless song.

Beside the river
        two children are gasping
at a paper boat
        swamped by stones.

Yellow

The weed has no mind,
except what I lend it, there
between two concrete slabs,
growing flowers so yellow
they burn in my sight, remain
long after I close my eyes,
as if I might see them in death,
smoking torches, sulphurous
beacons, guiding me on their
tough green stalks, lighting
the damp walls of the cave,
itself a borrowed mind, thinking
what stones must think when wet—
thinking sparks from flint,
thoughts about sharpening metal,
thinking what concrete thinks
when tree roots whisper deep down,
conspiring against its underside,
first a crack, then a gap,
a birthing ground for seed dust
to take hold, and rain to fill,
and then a stalk emerges, popping
buds, which become the living
thoughts of yellow beyond yellow.

Robert Peake read English at UC Berkeley and his poems have appeared in *California Quarterly, Cider Press Review, North American Review* and *Rattle*.

Valerie Lynch

Grandma wasn't often seen in 22 Garfield Street, Watford North

From inside her button box
the waterfall of metal and bone tumbled
over the moss-covered rocks of my left hand.

Most of grandma lived in the briskness of Dorset hills
those bare-backed horses maned with grass outside Powerstock.
Here she was born. Watched for adders under her feet

and friends who lay in the grass, talked to them in Dorset biscuity chunks.
Worked with the sun's fat clock
that ticked when it wanted and never published regulations.

Night of the Full Milk Moon

The vegetables bubbled and hissed in the iron pot,
and the wind came whistling, sniffing out

the sharpness of onions. The scent
of half-awake woman was spiked with the tang

of fresh-mown grass where they'd lain
in the meadow below, and he still laboured.

The sun blew roses into her body, open to him
as the night they'd slid on the bed that was new

in the full Milk Moon, when he leapt up and rushed out
to his lambs, big with songs that tossed him over the hills.

Valerie Lynch has had a varied career, from lecturing in economics and in archaeology, to Keeper of Archaeology in a City Museum; from 1984 she has worked as a psychotherapist.

Moments from a trench-career

After Edmund Blunden, Undertones of War

i

I wasn't eager to go
to the bombing-school near Paradis,
but learned to tramp the muddy roads,
to live in trenches, wash
in a biscuit-tin.

ii

We stared into confusion.
From the firesteps tried our longest throws
with Mills bombs
- like unlucky boys
whose game of ducks and drakes
turned one day serious.

iii

Few people on the streets of Ypres,
but the red post-office remained,
advertisements for Sunlight Zeep,
for Singer's Naaimachinen,
and fragments of the cathedral gateway
where parchment of old music lay
scattered amongst legless wicker chairs.

iv

Shells burst around us with a flat
pattering percussion of continual sound.
Then silence, and the solitude recaptured
a wilderness of windowed walls.

v
The open space all through the Salient
was crammed with men,
with animals, with transport.
Like a circus-ground.

vi
Port Arthur where we found
amongst the broken spades and empty tine
a muddy pair of soldier's boots
– still containing someone's feet.

vii
Our cheerful young lance-corporal
was making tea that afternoon.
                              A shell
dropped on a sudden from blue sky.
I turned, and when the smoke dispersed
the boy was gobbets of black flesh,
the earthwall sotted with his blood.
Bits of pulpy bone. A single eye
stared from the duckboard.

viii
Another dawn, and rain.
We trudged ahead.
The latest German missile
with a shriek burst over us,
exploded in the mud,
rocked all the earth around,
the air itself.
My twenty-first year
had come and gone
with mud, and gas,
and high explosives.

Bad Weather: For Isaac Rosenberg

God's castaway, the clumsy clown,
all but a derelict from Cable Street,
he'd known bad weather from the first.

No one could deny he had a gift
- though not for living: as for that
his card already had been marked.

An absent-minded very raw recruit,
he fought the drizzle and the lice
as much as Germans for his patch of sun,

for summer and the sweeter times
who'd lived in Nomansland already
when walking the Whitechapel streets,

when it was always far, so very far
from here, wherever here would be,
to the British Museum.

Unwritten epics lay beyond the ridge.
They rose before him like the Cambrai spires
glimpsed indistinctly through the mist

- a mist as thick as the tobacco-smoke
that climbed so high above the marble tables
to the painted ceiling of the Café Royal.

There is no hope of writing poems now.
Lost in the fog, all his defences smashed
he falls into a churned-up sea of mud

that welcomes yet another hapless guest,
its April fool, although the weather
shows - too late - some signs of clearing.

Prague: The Old Jewish Cemetery

It's impressed into a narrow strip of land
between the Klaus synagogue
and the Ceremonial Hall:

a confusion of tombs,
of crippled slabs aslant,
all higgledy-piggledy,

layer on layer, as if the dead
still like the living
jostled for the common air,

no space left in the damp black earth,
and all around the silence of
the all-but-vanished ghetto.

new soil sprinkled over each fresh grave
for yet another newly dead,
rituals repeated over centuries.

Bordellos, farriers' huts are gone,
the dog-catchers, outcasts, executioners
of the fifteenth century,

ghetto-hovels all burnt down
by order of a hygiene-minded emperor,
so nothing else in Josefov

can echo what lies here:
the bourgeois streets
deafen with their silence.

Smiling tourists at the gate
queue, pay their admittance charge
for a ticket that won't save their souls

but will give them pause
to gaze on teetering headstones,
the outnumbering dead,

where but for accidents of time and place
they must lie here too forgotten
confined in a crowded space.

Roger Caldwell writes as literary critic and philosopher for numerous journals. He has published two collections of poetry, *This Being Eden* (Peterloo Press) and *Walking on the Moon* (Ninth Arrondissement Press).

Clearing

Beneath conifers and cloudy skies
where the scent of sandalwood lingers
girls trail in silken swathes
carrying wood from the shrinking forest

children sift through cones and needles
trace the roots of the banyan tree
wonder at the buried fossils
withered leaves and rotting stumps

hunt for lost treasures savaged and axed
when the rasp of a chain-saw
sent tigers running for cover
silenced the monkeys, startled the gaur

clipped the wings of the kestrel in flight
cleared the hills to grow tea and rice
split the world of the tribes asunder
Toda, Kota, Irula, Kurumba

but picturesque images can be downloaded
at the press of a button
in black and white, sepia or colour
birdsong and music in quadraphonic

though the cries of the people
went unrecorded
drowned out by the sound of the saw
the thundering hooves of the buffalo

In the same time zone

when the dance began
clasped together like the hands
of a clock

now I can't place the hour

except your postcards
say it must be summer

the letters in the eaves
tell me I'm in Paris
you're in Brazil
poles apart –
back together
laughing in spring snow

surfing through foam
riding the same wave

before you know it
two birds flutter down
from the ash tree
wither into autumn leaves
settle on the garden seat

you throw off your boots
rucksack at your feet

I can't place the hour

don't need a watch
to track your footsteps
in the winter stars

Angela Croft has had poems published in *South Bank Poetry* (Issues 2 & 3).

Heroes

'The pony jerks and the riot's on.'
(From 'Clearances': Seamus Heaney)

Tromping to Monsalhead and back with friends,
you pause near dank cold Demonsdale beneath
a fitful crowded sky, mapping your mood
where Devil's Scabious turns green banks haze-blue
parade of Heroes, the Olympic dream
fulfilled: no lives at risk from those who fight
(Afghanistan, Iraq), or those who don't,
no bones wrong – right; no loving sacrifice.

Take Heaney's great-grandmother, off to Mass
in her new husband's trap for the first time,
mobbed by the Orange gang she'd left behind.
Sense neighbourly outrage, well-hurled insult,
riding the Troubles straight through here and now,
white knuckled cobbles, blood across the page.

Beneath Red Hill
In memory of Ed Wright

i

On holiday, long summer haul, fifteen,
I call on you, tight cobbled space behind
the cinema where Saturdays, aged eight,
from ten-fifteen, I queue for matinees
with mates, clock grainy old B western films.
Blisters my badge of pride, I yearn to be
like you, a working man in your flood prime.
Tarmac and dustcart gangs all take the piss.
I burn brick red. You ride as Tom Mix would.
"Tough sod but fair, Fred Wright," Jack Jenks has said.

ii

That stroke draws all your pride, word-shy, grid-locked
with concentration and embarrassment.
You know about the embolism, tick
on, borrow time - yet never tell your wife.
Talk tunes to old times you relent, restore
now bristling Lichfield Street, "A mere dirt track
for cart and carriage" where the nouveaux-riche
with Rolls or Bentley, bottle banks at Stoke,
build villas, ride to hounds, rough-shoot, a short
train ride from enterprise, slum-killing smoke.

iii

Low Anglican among massed Catholics,
a martyr to hard drink, I watch him edge
to your graveside. Their holy water words
well-spread, crumbs rap the coffin, like raised fists
on angry doors. "Sound bloke, your Uncle Fred."
Your education life, your geometry
the perfect squaring of a garage base,
you've earned your neighbourly footprint, know how
folks tick; part of your signature, your firm
handshake, the solid ground beneath my feet.

Peter Branson, a former Writer-in-residence for "All Write" has been published by journals including *Acumen, Ambit, Envoi, Fire, The Interpreter's House, Red Ink* and *Other Poetry*.

Bodysurf

To understand everything about the swell—
how on a given day the seventh in the cycle
provides the greatest chance to ride to shore
if caught where the rip collides with the surge,
where the wave pries a mouth wide
and prepares to heave its travelled miles—
to understand the moment of submission,
when to dive in and up the crest
in order to avoid a rabid tumble,
flung skyward out the other side
falling yards into the trough and humbled—
to understand that we're aligned
to leave behind horizons to the climbing wall,
hunched and turned three quarters,
believing that the travelling momentum
is such we'll be absorbed and pulled along—
so someone watching oceans from a towel
might raise herself a little on one elbow
and to her partner whisper, *Dolphins.*

Counterpoint

—after Conor O'Callaghan

Place something on the windowsill
before we get to swallows in the evening sky,
something between you and the sovereignty of air:
week-old roses, silver-framed relations,
or an old milk jug, chipped Cornish ware.
You choose, but it should be noted
as you're opening the mail, look up,
and make a little from the fact it's framed
by more than fabric: hand-washed nets become
the history of lace as it pertains to family,
or in that vein, the fading luxuries of velvets.
And as the swallows flit, of course like memories,
here you'll neatly segue to your close,
recall old dialogues, spot the stranger passing.

Paul Maddern was born in Bermuda and now lives in Co. Down. His work has appeared in various journals and anthologies and he's working towards a first collection.

Desperate Measures

She bends backwards
further than the chisel needs
hammers hard
and a line extends across his chest
cracking apart his heart.

Dust lines her sticky lungs.

She hacks him into chunks
litters the floor with his jumble of limbs
now and then she unearths a wink, a cheek,
a frightened lip.

Slice

Between biting his burger
and talking to her,
he stops at the kerb
of Gerald Street,
and they hover on the cusp
of the pavement.

She tells him to ignore everything.
He smiles at her,
squeezes tomato pips between his teeth
slides them through gaps,
wraps them around his front teeth
and licks them away without a thought.

He is far away
with the other girl he's been kissing
and the lips that cradle the burger
have been trailing her body for days.

Abegail Morley's first collection is *How to Pour Madness into a Teacup* (Cinnamon, December 2009); she appears in *The Sandhopper Lover* (Cinnamon). She won the Cinnamon Press Poetry Collection Award 2008.

Silver Ghosts

Silver ghosts gleaming in the meadow
like butterflies
                    with razorblade wings
sniffing for pollen
            pink as pure blow—
thereof,
            and more,
                        the poet will sing

Like butterflies with razorblade wings,
slash the clouds into bloody twilight
(thereof, also, the poet must sing),
once again suck the air of black night

Slash the clouds
            into bloody twilight,
celebrate all the dead in their graves,
once again breathe the air of black night—
poems come, furious,
                    in light-waves

Celebrate
            all the dead in their graves,
sniffing for pollen pink as pure blow,
poems come, furious, in light-waves:
silver ghosts,
                    gleaming in the meadow

Primates

His eyes intimate knowledge, this chimpanzee,
sparkling with the iron light of sentience,
we will have to expand our conception of the word
      HUMAN,
he is maybe the poet of his tribe and wizened
leader whom the others in the photo silently acquiesce to,
his mind forms open lines of hairy thought
knitted in his point in time and forest order

I, again, am alone in the mirror,
older now, a delicate cracking around the eyes,
nail-head pupils and my lashes are a mess,
this is not a photo but an instant never reoccurring
eternal, 3:10 A.M. between golden bathroom walls—
      sapience: unknown—
this face so secretly and fiercely familiar,
I will open another can of beer now but

tomorrow I will kill the poachers
      / I will murder the colonists
      / I will cut down the loggers
      / I will exterminate all the brutes

Grab the Polaroid

Grab the Polaroid
and head down to where they spray graffiti
on brick walls
and piss in alleys

the canal flows nearby
clogged with dead leaves of limitless autumns,
sometimes with suicides—
I mean that wasn't no dream
when you saw the police at the iron railing
looking down

or instead the river's mouth
at high tide a vast black pool,
cormorants wrestle with writhing eels,
     light glints
           on rubbery scales
     iron-blue beak
          swallows alive

don't drop off the edge of the
               earth

Michael S. Begnal is the author of three poetry collections: *AncestorWorship* (Salmon, 2007), *Mercury, the Dime* (Six Gallery Press, 2005), and *The Lakes of Coma* (Six Gallery Press, 2003). He is published in the anthology *Breaking the Skin: New Irish Poetry* (Black Mountain Press, 2002).

Interviews

George Szirtes

was born in Budapest in 1948 and came to England as a refugee in 1956. His thirteen books of poems include, *The Slant Door* (1979, winner of the Faber Prize), *Bridge Passages* (1991, short listed for the Whitbread Prize), *Reel* (2004, winner of the TS Eliot Prize) and *New and Collected Poems* (2008). He is also the prize-winning translator of a number of books of poetry and fiction from the Hungarian. A study of his work, *Reading George Szirtes*, by John Sears, was published by Bloodaxe in 2008. He was elected a Fellow of the Royal Society of Literature in 1982 and is associate editor of *The Liberal* and *Atlas* magazines. He currently teaches on the MA in Creative Writing at UEA.

You have a tremendously wide range of written work; poetry, translations, articles, essays and librettos. When something attracts your attention, at what point do you know it will be a poem rather than something else?

That is not too difficult really. Librettos and articles generally have some external origin. Someone asks me to write them, and I generally do my best to oblige. I wouldn't confuse either with a poem, though libretti do contain verse and, sometimes, set song. I usually spend a long time preparing those then write very fast, rewriting afterwards. I can't write slowly. Articles and essays require organisation of a different sort, generally of reference material and broad ideas that might then spring off more specific ones. Nice to see where they lead.

Translations are again set and commissioned, Novels are just for getting on with. Poems

vary. There are some poets I simply can't do. I don't fully get what they are doing. Once I know I move relatively fast again. Novels go in fits and starts.

Poems are a feeling waiting for a first line. They can be summoned on good days.

I am interested in your process: can you say what triggers or calls into being that first line, or what it is that allows you to summon them 'on good days'?

The trigger for the first line is usually an impression of something over and beyond the normal. It might be unusual in itself, or simply ordinary but somehow more intense. Triggers vary in type of course, but it is as if the act of perceiving a trigger - and, to some degree, we half-consciously train ourselves to perceive such things - were a kind of opening into latencies behind the first impression.

Triggers are, for me at least, also various forms of escape from the general insensateness of life, the usual life that demands concentrated attention on business of one sort or another. It's probably not surprising then that my first poems, such as they were, were, almost always, diversions from duty. Studying physics at school for example, I'd stop doing my homework and start a poem. A concentrated effort in one direction seemed glad to jump tracks into another. Or maybe the substantial burden of the one became the potential substance of the other: a kind of equivalence and of course the attention was partly in and through language, the language not required by any of my academic subjects: physics, zoology and chemistry.

Again quite personally, because I am aware

that other poets feel quite differently, I have often found that being asked to write about something can trigger exactly the same process. A commission is, for me, another form of opening. The burden of conceiving a subject from scratch is shifted to the given subject. It is as if a certain undetermined, directionless, stored energy that might have remained trapped and indecisive (approaching, in extreme cases, the condition we call 'writer's block') were delighted to take whatever outlet happened to be on offer.

The given is often the surprising, and surprise is important. For that reason I have never liked the smell of poems that seem to know from the very start where they are headed. I suspect they are not real poems, the genuine poetic act being marked by a series of surprises, presented by, negotiated in and discovered through language.

You use poetic forms with skill and, it seems to me as a reader, have a relaxed relationship with the formal elements of poetry. Do you feel form facilitates the conditions that allow the series of surprises which signal "the genuine poetic act"?

Yes, I do feel form offers surprises. My argument for it would be based less on issues of tradition or completion (that some would call closure) or even the part-mystical case put forward by some of the New Formalists, that meters approximate to key natural or body rhythms, though I think there is something valuable in that perception. I would argue from language. The normal speech act treats language as though it hardly existed, or was in some way transparent. You want to say something: you say it. Language in poetry, I feel, is more physically present. It offers resistance. You have to negotiate it, like a strong wind blowing in your face. Rhymes, meters, stanza forms, almost anything that constitutes opposition or constraint, brings the sheer materiality of language to notice. You cannot entirely have your own way with it. In negotiating it you are taken where you might not otherwise

go. So you discover it as you go. There are many analogies I could use to illustrate this, but if I were to stick to the idea of the strong headwind, then the act of writing would be like tacking when sailing. That tacking, that negotiation, improvisation and surprise route is, I suspect, at the heart of the poetic act. The act need not necessarily involve any specific set of formal problems, maybe the sheer awareness of the wind is enough. One thing of which I am convinced: poetry is not a matter of having something to say then saying it.

You have drawn comparisons, on your blog, between poems and photographs; particularly "of the lyric poem as the capturing of a landscape or event as lit by lightning" and explain further that "it comes about through the perceived sense of connection between language and the sense of reality. The connection feels electric. The two poles of what we say and what there is seem, briefly, to coincide." This seems closely connected to the importance of surprise you note above; it also suggests an urgency about writing poetry. Can that urgency be denied? You clearly lead a very busy life: how do you manage the demanding energy of a poem waiting to be written?

It is odd how these images occur in the mind. The lightning-lit landscape or event isn't one I have used before but once it appeared it seemed perfectly convincing. The image came when I was looking for ways of explaining to a huge group of students how they might read a longer poem, as opposed, say, to a novel. It has been suggested before that the long poem is essentially a series of short poems strung together. I am not sure that is right in every respect, because epic poetry clearly has a strong sense of narrative flow, so when EV Rieu, for example, translates Homer as prose, it seems perfectly natural. There do remain, of course, those transitional passages between main episodes that are less intense, but those exist in prose narrative too. In lyric poetry we expect language to do more with less. We expect intensity of effect and a long poem that is not essentially epic will probably consist of a series of brightnesses with minimal use of functional connecting verse. The analogy I wanted was between poems as photographs and novels as feature-length films. That is not perfect since clearly there is a sense of happening in lyric poems: something is different by the end, so the idea of seeing something in the conditions of an electric storm presented itself. You see figures moving or fleeing or dancing, and everything is bright, then they've gone, leaving you only with the sense of significance. That lightning, I argued, was generated by the power gathered in language as density, as materiality, as a substance. You can feel the air thicken before a storm. It's like that.

Can the urgency be denied? I don't want to suggest that the condition of the poet is necessarily to be permanently set in a Romantic attitude, ravished by lightnings. It is the effect of the poem I mean, not the poet's psychic state or the mode of composition. In arguing to the students I suggested that the phrases we use, such as 'sheer poetry' and 'poetry in motion' tend to be applied to brief movements or acts of grace. That that is, if you like, our visceral definition of poetry. It is perfectly possible for poets to feel calm, cool, even cold and rational, and, under those circumstances, to write slowly. But the effect they are working towards is that lightning-lit pool of words that seems to correspond with the density of one's sense of life. That is why Housman felt the hairs on the back of his neck rise, that is why Marianne Moore's imaginary gardens have real toads in them. That is the magic of the poetic shape.

As concerns my own experience there is, I think, a vague sense of a thickening of the air before the poem begins. The rest is a matter of heading into that language-wind the best I can. It is the way I have always written, from the very beginning. One can train oneself to be aware of the thickening. One can do it by an act of concentration. Because the thickening is everywhere, in any subject, at any moment. It is, as with all art, a matter of intense attention. I started writing poetry as distraction from the pressures of writing up experiments in physics at eighteen. Pressure can go a long way to thickening the available air. I work well under pressure.

The comparison between photography and poetry, as well as the fleeting nature of lightning, suggest freezing a moment in time. Do you see poetry as an attempt to capture or freeze time?

I think I probably did see it that way, certainly through much of my earlier work. Now I would say the photograph analogy - forgive me repeating myself here - is not quite comprehensive enough, because there is, and has to be, movement of some sort in a poem, otherwise it's just description. So a very brief pocket of time containing everything relevant before and after and during is probably the ideal. I think I could make a case for that in the lyric poetry of almost any time. I think I could: it's just a hunch now.

You have said, elsewhere, that you write poetry quickly, that you can't write slowly: is this true also of revision or re-writing? Can you describe your process up to the point where you know a poem is ready for publication?

Revision can take time, indeed a long time, but it depends. I have grown up being my own editor and am not always right. Many times I would have loved a tough but understanding editor to quarrel with. However, one has to be one's own editor to some degree, probably for over 90% of the process. I read my poems aloud. I read them to Clarissa, my wife, who, though she is primarily a visual artist, has a good sharp ear. And even if she didn't, her listening sharpens my ear. I usually advise poets to read their work to someone else, just so they themselves hear it with the consciousness of an external presence. Occasionally I will let the computer read one of my shorter poems from Simple Text. In the past I have had friends, other poets, to whom I have showed new work. It wasn't the group dynamic of the workshop but the sense of one mind addressing another without any social distraction. I have been lucky with friends. One needs a series of them. I do it mostly for myself now and this is, in a way, liberating but it is also risky. However, I am now of the age when I think risks are the best friends. How do I know when a poem is ready for publication? I guess. And hope. And, like anyone else, I suppose, trust to instinct, knowing it is not infallible.

Finally, I'd like to refer to your 2005 TS Eliot Lecture: I was struck by the truth of the ice skating metaphor and by the recognition of the moment of stepping on to the ice. You said that, rather than a linear apprenticeship, there is "a particular point at which the nature of poetry is understood for the first time. That first step on to the ice involves understanding both the point of the ice and something of ice's nature." As a teacher, do you think students can be helped on to the ice, or can you only provide the signposts towards it?

Yes, I do believe so, otherwise I wouldn't have been teaching all this time. The fact is I have seen this happen many times over. A lot of my ex-students have gone on to publications and awards of one sort or another, among them a good number who had not considered themselves poets or even readers of poetry when they started. Understanding poetry is like suddenly seeing the point of something that has always been there.

It is an extraordinary experience watching this happen to people and enormously cheering because it demonstrates that poetry is not some minor decorative art or an abstruse science but something bred in the bones. That it is a natural and fundamental human concern.

The point about poetry is that it is as true to life (and by life I mean imagination as well as experience) as we know to be in the medium of language, whether that truth be simple, complicated, personal or public. It doesn't matter what the context is. It is the voice speaking about the world, singing the world as best it can.

The biggest mistake people make about poetry is to think of it as concerned only with specific feelings felt only by peculiarly sensitive people. The issue is not with feeling but with language: the feeling arises out of the language, through the language. People do actually recognise this once presented with it in contexts other than poetry. That is part of teaching too.

The ice image in the Eliot Lecture arose out of Edmund Blunden's poem, The Midnight Skaters, where the pond is murky, deep and dangerous, but the skaters are exhorted to wheel across its thin, brittle surface in full knowledge of its fragility. The ice, in my reading, is language: the deep pond, the mass of inchoate experience in which we might well drown. Dancing on the ice is making patterns in language, making marks on it. Poetry is the pattern that gives meaning to the ice, that confirms and shapes it.

Beginning to hear the world through / in language is the stepping out on the ice. Students can, of course, be helped on to it. But first we must try to give them some idea of what the ice is for and what might be done on it. That is a matter of listening and watching. First we should become good readers: good listeners and watchers. To read well is a prerequisite: you cannot write well if you don't read well. Reading can be enough for many people. Sometimes I think it might be enough for me. But then it isn't. I have a vocation. Teaching poetry is not necessarily about preparing students for a vocation. It is not career guidance. It is introducing them to that which they feel anyway.

The poetic vocation is the sense of moving across that ice and wanting to move across it for ever.

Interview by Angela France

The Burning of the Books

Prologue

When he had gathered all the books

When he had indexed, catalogued, cross-referred and annotated them
When the little princelings and mighty emperors of China
Were dancing on the pinpoint of his own estimable head
And the bile of the world was swimming in the gutters
And the fists of the janitor were beating street girls black and blue
And the oleaginous salesman had lubricated the hinges of the *cassone*
For the delectation of the housekeeper
A tiny gale started blowing
Down the alleyways and through the portals
Through the flightless windows
Through the wainscoted corridors of the *rathaus*
And the Groszbeggars stirred and shook a leg
And the Dixwounded rattled their small change of limbs
And acrobats stood on their heads like stars
And there were murders
Murders and conspiracies
For the intellect to catalogue and classify
For the mind to annotate and the fingers to cross-refer
For a superior consciousness to make sense of
In the hallways and beer cellars
In the prisons and surgeries
In lavatories and libraries

Where the books were gathered.

2. In tall angular letters

Where books are gathered there gathers also the dust
That sieves through the pores of the skin and the head
The absolute dust of the language that falls apart
In your hands, that settles in your palm
Like a promise. Ideas are dust. Words dust,
A universe of dust between planet and planet,
Precious dust certainly, gold dust, a dusting
Of light filtered through eyelashes batting over
The damp-smelling page, the foxing, the marginals,
The improvised shopping list of the dead,
The dead themselves, the dust of the prisons,
The workhouses of dust, the dust bowl, the dustbin
Of history, the dust of the poor who have wasted away
Into particles, molecules, atoms, the dust of the birds
In their nests, the dust of the hotel where the dwarf
And the scholar fossick among motes
Among invisible books, the books of the imagination,
The trapped dust of the folded page, the folded umbrella,
The folds of the skin that are clogged with dust,
The dust of the ovens to come, the dust of the scouring pad,
The citizens of dust in the dusty streets
The dust of the city you shake off your sandals
The dust mites, the silverfish of the imagination,
The dust of the station where a speech is in progress,
The dust of the mountain pass with its butchered soldiers.
        Librarian of the universal library, have you explored
The shelves in the stockroom where the snipers are sitting,
The repository of landmines in the parking bay
The suspicious white powder at the check-out desk
The mysterious rays bombarding you by the photocopier
The psychological disorder of the filing system
That governs the paranoid republic of print
In the wastes of the world?

3. She opened the book and read

Once she had passed over the kid gloves
And the book appeared with its antiquary bloom
Its insect words pinned into place with light
It was clear there was expense involved.
Expense and respect, and a question of property.
I don't deal with property. I am a scholar.
I don't do housekeeping. I don't do money.
I do the rounds of the bookshops, interrogating
Dealers with rare editions in long-lost languages.
I have circumnavigated the alleys of Berlin
More often than I can remember, but I recall
Perfectly the place of each book on each shelf
And have marked its neighbours and condition.
Money is air. I breathe it in and out.
I blow my nose clear of it. I piss it in the morning
And last thing at night. Money is the slight breeze
Playing round my temples as I enter the shop,
The slight draught at my back as I leave it.
It is a whisper of fallen leaves in the gutter
The rustle half-dry and half-damp of a system in decay.
Pass me the kid gloves. I am handling a book.
The words of the dead are settling over me.
I drift among them, weightless, like a balloon
Floating on helium, looking down on gutters
Overflowing with leaves and paper money.
I don't see the difference.

Taken from the title sequence of George Szirtzes' new collection
The Burning of the Books (Bloodaxe, 2009).

Katrina Porteous

is a poet and historian, born in Aberdeen and now based on the Northumberland coast. She has been Writer-in-Residence in the Shetland Islands and at the Aldeburgh Poetry Festival, has written many long poems for BBC Radio, and is President of the Northumbrian Language Society. Her publications include *The Lost Music, The Wund an' the Wetter, The Bonny Fisher Lad, Dunstanburgh, Longshore Drift* and *The Blue Lonnen*.

Much of your work seems concerned with that which is passing away — occupations, way of life, language: how important is it to you that these things are recorded in poetry as well as in history books?

I should say that I've chosen my subjects — primarily inshore fishing (*The Lost Music, The Wund an' the Wetter, Longshore Drift, The Blue Lonnen*), but also coal mining (in *Turning the Tide*), hill farming and other threatened or vanishing industries of the North East — because they are the industries which have created the culture of the people and places I love. We live at a time of accelerated social and economic change. The cultural distinctions of 40 years ago — class, identity, belonging — have altered beyond recognition. I am not nostalgic or sentimental about this. My mother's family came from a Durham colliery village and I would not wish to return to the conditions of that community in the mid 20th century, nor to those of a fisherman or his wife at the time of the long-lines. But I am also deeply aware that rapid change in the lives of people and communities can leave a sense of loss — of direction or identity or political will. It is to this sense of loss, in the people among whom I live, that my poems are addressed. I write for them primarily, and not for a 'poetry' audience.

Having said that, I can answer your question very simply. Poetry is more important to me than history books. That is true in spite of the fact that I chose to study history at university, and in spite of the fact that I've written prose history books as well. Prose history is a record of something past or passing; a signpost to experience, to which it is more or less faithful. But because poetry is, to me, primarily spoken and heard rather than read on the page, it is alive in the present; at its best, I believe that it has the power to invoke its subject — to bring something of its subject into the presence of speaker and listener.

That is not to say that poetry has any immediate power to change the world or, in Auden's sense, to make anything 'happen'; writing poems about vanishing fishing communities cannot prolong their life. But I do profoundly believe that the shared act of speaking and listening to poetry, itself creates a communality in which something of the subject can be made present. Perhaps it is simply a matter of taking the listener for a moment into the fisherman's consciousness; how he feels, how he thinks, insofar as I can understand those things. That is done through primitive and largely unconscious means of sound, rhythm and relations of likeness and unlikeness, familiarity and surprise.

Poetry is an act of concentrated listening, not only for the person who hears the poem, but, more importantly, for the poet. If the poem is to work, the poet must really listen, with every sense, during the act of writing. It is a matter of being as true as possible to the subject — a complicated matter, as I'll try to explain later, but at the same time an intensely simple one. The result is that if the poem is true, if it is faithful to its subject and to itself, it will invoke its subject in the presence of its listeners, and keep its subject present in a way that no history book ever could.

There is also the simple fact that a poem, unlike a history book, is portable in the head. It belongs to whoever claims it. For this reason, in spite of its reputation, poetry is actually potentially less 'elitist' than prose, and more subversive. I think of it, at least partly, as belonging to the tradition of popular song. I like the sense of the poem as a living germ which can be passed on and spread, creating its own community. This is, I believe, in the deepest sense, a political act as well as an aesthetic one. A poem can act upon people's consciousness, help us think about who we are, where we have come from, where we are heading.

Writing in dialect is undeniably challenging: it often results in an unintentionally comic effect or can seem patronising; the fishermen poems in 'The Lost Music' are neither of these. Can you say something about what made the dialect work for you?

I was extremely lucky to catch a generation of fishermen and women among whom the Northumbrian dialect still had its full expressive range and integrity. I spent years immersed in their conversation, listening to them for several hours every day, and it was only as I began that total immersion that I began to write properly in dialect. Twenty years later, I hear much less dialect spoken around me. I can still write in it when I try, but I have to get back to that place in my head where I hear it; and that takes considerable concentration and effort now that I no longer hear it outside.

You're right that dialect can have an unintentionally patronising or humorous effect. I think that there are several reasons for this. One is the obvious inherited issue of class and power – the assumption that the 'educated' speaker is in some way 'superior' to the dialect speaker. Dialect speakers themselves, of course, were traditionally made to feel 'inferior' at school and taught to 'speak properly'. Many in the 20th century were in fact bilingual, and used the dialect as a kind of glue within their own community or subversively (when they did not want to be understood by outsiders).

A second reason why I think a dialect might seem unintentionally humorous might be to do with its sounds. Briefly, the sounds of Northumbrian dialect connect very viscerally with the things they describe. There is almost no need to consult a glossary when you hear

words like 'claggy', 'scaddit', 'snell' used in context. They contain their meaning in their own music. We understand them, not just with our heads, but with all our physical senses.

A third problem in using dialect which may give rise to unintended humour is that of juxtaposition. As 'standard English' and dialect represent two very different sorts of music, familiar and unfamiliar, they do not sit well together. This becomes a problem when the writer only has a limited vocabulary of dialect words at her disposal, which she has somehow to try to shoehorn into standard speech patterns. It is less of a problem when the integrity of the dialect is intact – when it still has a wide vocabulary and distinct speech rhythms and is, essentially, a separate language. The problem then is to be sufficiently immersed in it to be able to use it consistently.

If popping a few dialect words or (worse) grammatical constructions into a standard English line just doesn't work, oddly (and probably related to the first point about class), it perhaps works better the other way round. One of the best-known Northumbrian dialect poets was Fred Reed, but when you look at his work closely you'll see that there is always a pull towards using polysyllabic, non-dialect words and cadences whenever he gets 'serious'. This does not have the humorous effect that dropping dialect into standard English has; but I think that it could be said to weaken his poetry.

In many of my own poems about the fishermen in 'The Lost Music' I avoided the problems inherent in the juxtaposition of my language with theirs, and that of issues of authority, by deliberately using two separate voices 'in conversation' within one poem. Because the dialect speakers were the ones with the knowledge and wisdom, and I was their ignorant student, any comic effect in the dialect was subverted – they were in the position of authority, not I.

A further potential problem with dialect, which I often encounter when judging dialect poetry competitions at Northumberland shows, is the tendency for particular patterns of rhythm to set themselves up for comic effect. It is very hard to express anything serious in a sing-song anapaestic nursery-rhyme meter; much better to listen to the patterns of the speech itself, and to allow those to shape the form of the verse.

Your juxtaposition of natural and industrial imagery in a number of poems creates an effect that is both striking and poignant; where does a poem start for you? Is it with an image, an idea or something else?

A poem for me is an intensely physical thing, which starts from a bodily, emotional sensation of wanting to be elsewhere. It is a feeling not unlike desire, or nostalgia, or yearning; except that the object of the feeling is unknown. So that's the necessary cause. In order to get there, there has also to be a sufficient cause; and that, to me, is also physical: a pattern of sounds – or more usually a number of these – which take the form of phrases. Often these may be visual or other sense images at the same time; but the important thing is that they must sound – must reverberate in some way, so that other sounds may grow out of them. The key to getting it right is that all these physical elements – the emotion and the sound patterns and the sense images – should converge, strike up unexpected echoes in one another, and transport you to the elsewhere you somehow suspected was there all along.

You refer to a juxtaposition of natural and industrial imagery in my work, which you find poignant perhaps because it contains contradictory or paradoxical qualities. The processes of coal-mining, for example, and the separation and sifting of its waste, so cruelly destructive to nature (and people), are themselves chemical and geological processes dependent upon natural forces. Similarly, an invasive industry like steel production is in constant dia-

logue with a natural world which it seemingly destroys, but which re-colonises and undoes the human at every opportunity. You're right that these subtle negotiations between the human and the natural lie at the heart of my work. If I have any central, organising belief, it is in the human species as part of nature; often and even principally a destructive part; but ultimately an instrument of nature, which has only one object – to change.

And change, this process of time which I find so endlessly fascinating, comes about by means of contradiction and paradox. The important thing to remember is that it is not the idea from which a poem begins, but the idea in which a poem ends. The experience of writing a poem is itself one of paradox. The first paradox is that, in order to build something out of words, you must first get rid of words completely. The second is that, in order to find the sounds that will do the work of the poem, you have to draw on all your other physical senses.

I will try to give you an example. To write the kind of poem to which you refer, about place, I would, wherever possible, go to that place; walk through it, observe it, touch it, smell it – listen with all the senses. For the poem 'Blackberries', I visited the site of Consett Ironworks, which I already knew well. To write the poem, which was a commission, it was not enough to remember it. I had to go there with my notebook, and spend a couple of hours, very quietly, listening; trying to empty my head of the clutter of words and associations, and to experience the small details of the place as if for the first time.

What I mean by getting rid of words is that, instead of looking at a bramble bush and saying 'bramble bush', which would immediately stop me seeing it, I looked at it as if it had no name – looked at its shapes and colours, its textures, its smells, the sounds it made – until it became an alien, utterly unfamiliar thing; and only then did I try to translate it back into words.

I did that again and again with many small concrete details of the place. My notebook was full of phrases like: 'they drag their barbed wires'; 'the sky is the colour of cold iron'; 'the dock rattles its seeds'. There were also a lot of observations which never made it into the poem. Some of them were good observations. But the fact is that when, several weeks later, I felt that sense of yearning, and started to write the poem, I looked in my notebook for phrases, and some of them took me somewhere musically and others did not. The ones that took me somewhere were the ones that made it into the poem. Let me rephrase that. They were the ones that made the poem; because their sounds were the germs of other sounds, and whatever sense imagery they contained set off other associations and reverber-ated with them and made chords and discords and harmonies.

Other poems have begun with phrases of speech. In the poem 'Charlie Douglas', for example, the line 'Aah'll tell ye somethin'. Now this is true...' was something Charlie regularly said in conversation. That and other phrases of his direct speech gave that poem its shape and energy. The most extreme example is 'The Wund an' the Wetter', which was built almost entirely out of phrases and words of recorded speech. I was commissioned to write a poem in dialect just at the time when many of Charlie's generation were dying. I therefore set out to include in that poem as many and much as I could of their words and speech. I trawled through hundreds of pages of transcriptions and notes that I'd made over the years from interviews, and hauled out phrases. My notebook contained lists of real speech expressions: 'Howway doon t' the churchyard an' ask the aa'd men'; 'Come wi' the wund an' gan wi' the wetter'; 'By, lad, she's a reight Taggarine man's haal!'. I then played around with these phrases until they set up musical associations with each other in my head. It was just like letting them talk to one another. I feel that

I contributed very little to that poem, other than, as it were, conducting the orchestra.

I'm sometimes asked about the difference between writing, as in 'The Wund an' the Wetter', in a 'dramatic' voice, and in 'my own' voice, as 'I'. In my experience, there is little difference. Of course, striving to be 'true' is essential to the poetic voice; but the truth, as we try to apprehend it, is by no means the same thing as autobiography or confession. It can be accessed through personae, multiple voices, dialogue, fictions, conceits, contradictions. I am not at all sure that I believe in the traditional distinction between the lyric and dramatic voice. To some extent, the lyric is always dramatic. I write in many voices, all of them in some sense dramatic, and all of them in some sense 'me'. The relationship of any one of those voices to the self is like that of a snapshot to time. Truth enacts itself in time, and is therefore only accessed through multiplicity, contradiction, the complex relation of parts to the whole.

In the poem 'Factory Girl', which is one of the earliest poems in 'The Lost Music' (1987), I use the image of beads threaded on a string to explore the idea of how we make narratives about our lives. That was a poem about making our histories; but it is also oddly descriptive of the way I write poetry, building poems out of scraps of speech or bits of observations, which could be threaded together in a multitude of different ways, but whose form is finally determined by sound association. In a way, that takes us back full circle, to your first question about poetry and history. For me, perhaps the two activities are ultimately the same: trying to find some kind of order, or beauty, within the chaos of experience.

Interview by Angela France

Cathy

'See yon heuk?' says Cathy.
'Yon's ma life.'
Three-quarters of an inch of steel,

Barbed at the hyeutter, bent,
It glitters
Like a jewel.

Tiny. Cathy, six stone, volatile as petrol,
Wiry, lean,
Puts on her shawl.

Pleased to see you, kettle on,
Deaf as a sharpening stone
To every sound

Except the wireless static crackle
From the boat,
A little whirlwind,

She pegs the sheets out in the backyard,
Scrubs the step, stirs the pan,
Swabs the floor –

'When fetther hord it was
Another girl
He slammed the door.

Aye, but
He couldn't dae wi'oot dowters, ye kna.'

Cathy, bent
Beneath the creel:
Home from the mussel beds, the limpet pool;

Six stone of haddocks haa'ked aroond Reed Raa',
Husband, in-laws, tugging at her, kin
Needing her care,

Mussels to skeyn,
The boat to launch, lines to bait, claes to poss,
Sons to bear;

Cathy, bent with pains,
Years; busy as a sanderling,
Never still,

Down the harbour with the barrow, eyes
Blue as the Coquet, bright
As steel,

As hard, as sharp, as necessary
As a fish-hook
To the house, the men;

Cathy, without whom
A coble could not go to sea — as vital to it
As diesel, or the wind.

Claes: clothes; Coble: traditional Northumbrian inshore fishing boat; Dowters: daughters; Haa'k: to sell from door to door; Heuk: a hook; Hyeutter: the barbed end of the hook; Lines: long lines, which carried up to 1,400 hooks, baited with mussels and limpets by fisher women; Poss: to beat clothes in water with a stick to wash them; Reed Raa': Red Row, a village near Amble, Northumberland; Skeyn: to shell, as mussels and limpets for bait.

Shanky

Shanky is all England:
A barn-conversion.
Strangers in four-by-fours. Forgotten

Names: the Butty Meadow. Shanky Hall.
The nugget of a chapel.
Faith in ruins.

Down the Long Nanny Burn
A green gate leans.
Dark, witchy hawthorns

Point along the leat
To Shanky Mill,
Its bricked-up windows, walls

Empty, its rafters open
To the swifts, the rain;
The knotted fabric of the farm

Shrunk, first, to one man
Alone in his tractor cabin,
Radio on; then

To no one
But the nostalgic, who like it here
At nightfall, when

Black cows wallow in the burn
And the low sun
Floods everything golden.

From *The Blue Lonnen, (Jardine Press 2007).*

Lovely Day

Vanishing,

          bobbing up,

                    vanishing,

                              north of the Buoy,

The Supreme dips and disappears in Beadnell bay,

Dark speck among mountainous seas of molten silver.

'Ye've missed your chance, now, Eddie. Lie where y' are.'

John's on the pier, on the wireless, winding him in.

'Now! Put some speed on!' She surges ahead. From behind,
A huge bruise-livid roller — *'Whoa! Eddie!'* — catches her stern

And heaves her —

               Yawing,

                        See-sawing —

                                      Towards the sun.

Down she slides, backwards, afloat still; the sea rolls on.

'Now, gan! Haa'd north a bit. Norrard.' Eddie turns her
Head to the pier, as the next surge carries her, riding —

Up, forward,

               Momentarily surfing —

                              Subsiding.

And suddenly she is through it, into flat water
And a pool of sun; and milky behind her
The shaken sea, the shock of the breaking waves.

On the pier, a woman walking her terrier, smiles:

'Hello John —

               Lovely day!'

Excerpt from: The Wund an' the Wetter

Aah can mind the time when the men wad stand
On the top a the bank lookin' oot for' the land,
An' the soond a theer crack was as good as a sang
As th' reeled off the marks th' had lorned for sae lang:
For' Langoth an' Collith t' Comely Carr,
For' the Bus a' the Born t' the Shad an' the Bar,
Faggot, the Styenny Hyels, Fiddler's Fyace,
The Cock Craa' Stoene an' thon hob-hard place
At Herrod's Hoose Plantin on Aa'd Weir's hut;
The Chorch on the Black Rock, wheer ye shoot
Sooth for' the smooth at the Benty Gut:
T' the Cundy Rock an' the trink i' the sand
Reight ablow Featherblaa' – by, she was grand.
Ye could listen aa' neet. Th' wore spells, them words –
The map an' the key tae the treasure hoard.
Noo gi' us the marks for t' finnd 'em ageyn;
Howway doon t' the chorchyard an' ask the aa'd men,

For it's come wi' the wund an' gan wi' the wetter –
We'll noe be wantin' 'em noo...

But t' heor 'em gollerin' ower a boat
Wi' the soonds a the Norsemen still thick i' theer throat –
For' carlin t' fishroom, inwaver t' crook,
Ye'll nivvor finnd these i' the page on a beuk –
Ah, but they're bonny, the pairts on a cowble –
Dip a' the forefoot, lang i' the scorbel,
For' tack heuk an' gripe t' the horns a' hor scut,
For hor thofts t' hor thowelds – th' had nyems for the lot
That unlocked a hyel world...

                              – Which is no t' forgit
The fagarrashin foond in a fisherman's hut –
(Ye'd say it could dae wi' a reight reed up!) –
Wi' pellets an' dookas an' pickets an' poys,
Swulls an' sweels an' bows for buoys,
Rowells an' bowelts an' barky sneyds,

The tyeble aa’ claed wi’ perrins a’ threed,
Wi’ hoppin’s an’ hingin’s tha’s toozled like tows,
An’ pokes for the whullicks, an’ bundles a skowbs,
An’ cloots for’ a dopper the caaldies ha’ chowed.

But hey – look oot! – divvin’t gan in theer:
Ye’ll nivvor git lowsed, ’cos she’s wizenbank fair!

It aa’ tummels oot in a roosty shoower;
The nets unraffle wi’ cloods a stoor.
Ye’re varnigh scumfished afore ye can caal
For the becket, the brailor, the ripper an’ aa’
The whuppin’s an’ leashin’s aback a the waa’ –
By, lad, she’s a reight taggarine-man’s haal!

An’ it’s nae bother – it’s naen
T’ shut the door on yon.
Put oot the light. Forgit the nyems,
We’ll nivvor be wantin’ them things ageyn –
It’s come wi’ the wund an’ gan wi’ the wetter –
We’ll noe be needin’ ’em noo...

Barky sneyds: snoods, attaching hooks to long lines, preserved with bark; *Becket*: loop of rope attached to pot; *Bowelts*: graithing bolt, used to drag for lost gear; *Brailor*: net on pole for scooping fish aboard; *Bus*: weedy rock; *Caaldies*: rats; *Carlin*: space forward in coble; *Cloot*: rag; *Cowble*: coble, Northumbrian boat; *Crack*: talk; *Crook*: forward timber inside coble; *Cundy*: drainage ditch; *Dooka*: large float; *Dopper*: oilskin; *Fagarrashin*: mess, upheaval; *Fishroom*: space amidships in coble; *Forefoot*: curved ‘keel’ forward in coble; *Gollerin’*: shouting; *Gripe*: narrowing of coble at bow; *Hingin’s*: twine attaching net to tow, south of Beadnell; *Hoppin’s*: same, in Beadnell; *Inwaver*: inner supporting timber of coble; *Leashin’s*: lashings; *Pellet*: small float; *Perrin*: bobbin; *Picket*: boat hook; *Poke*: bag; *Poy*: boat stick; *Reed up*: clear up; *Ripper*: double hand line; *Rowells*: rollers on side of coble; *Scorbel*: one of twin ‘keels’ aft in coble; *Scumfished*: smothered; *Scut*: upper plank at stern of coble; *Shad*: shallow place, bank; *Skowb*: cut stick for pot rails; *Stoor*: dust; *Sweel*: swivel for attaching buoy to pot; *Swull*: basket for long line; *Tack heuk*: place on coble’s bow to attach sail; *Taggarine-man*: tinker; *Thofts*: thwarts, seats in coble; *Thowelds*: thole pins for oars; *Tow*: rope; *Trink*: deep place in sand; *Wizenbank fair*: extremely messy; *Whullicks*: winkles; *Whuppin’s*: fastenings, bindings.

From: *The Wund an’ the Wetter*, (Iron Press) 1999.

Christopher James

has won The Bridport and Ledbury poetry prizes and in 2002 was the recipient of an Eric Gregory Award. Born in Paisley in 1975, he is a graduate of the Creative Writing MA at the University of East Anglia. His first collection, *The Invention of Butterfly,* was published in 2006 by Ragged Raven Press. He won this year's National Poetry Competition.

Firstly many congratulations on winning the National Poetry Competition 2008. You've won other poetry prizes, so I'm curious to know what impact you think winning a single poem competition may have, or has in the past had, in terms of the exposure of your work to a broader audience?

No matter what the impact, winning a big competition is certainly a lot of fun - there's adrenaline rush when you find out; the sudden affirmation it brings to what you are doing - all those late nights suddenly add up to something very worthwhile. The presentations are always a buzz too - they're a great chance to network (the famous Bridport prize winning banquet is handsome reward in itself) as well as giving you the chance to have your Oscar moment, if you're into such things. When I won my first couple of prizes, I rather naively thought doors would start swinging open for me - but you still have to have the consistently high quality of work to back it up. Shortly after winning my Gregory, I sent off to a couple of publishers, but just wasn't ready for a first collection - I didn't have enough good poems. It took another two or three years to assemble this. Probably the best thing of winning a single poem competition is that you do receive invites to read at festivals and events. I got the chance to read at Aldeburgh, Cheltenham and Ledbury which gave me a chance to perform for a highly discerning audience, including a masterclass with Paul Muldoon. And I've forgotten to mention the money (which always comes in handy for someone like me who always lives beyond their means . . .)

What are your thoughts, in general, about the widespread nature of competition in Poetry? I was thinking more about the difference this makes, in terms of re-engaging, connecting the majority of people with poetry, and in some way convincing them that poetry still has significance, and a relevance in the contemporary and real world we live in?

I think competitions give people a good snapshot of what's happening in poetry, in as much as that is possible. However I would be careful not to overstate the case for the amount of fame a single poem can win - it takes years for even a prize winning poem to make an impression in the popular consciousness, as opposed to say, a big hit single, which the public embrace collectively and immediately. You hear stories about 18th century poems making such an impression, but it's difficult to imagine again. Perhaps it was last achieved by Larkin or Heaney in both the popular and literary sense? I think for the most part, competition websites and anthologies are read more by other poets than the public. Perhaps the National Poetry Competition and the Arvon competition are the exceptions because of national newspaper coverage. On the whole, while competitions are good ways to draw attention to current work, I think probably radio has a bigger part to play in keeping contemporary poetry alive. While the public is much smarter now, and will be familiar with Simon Armitage, Andrew Motion, Carol Ann Duffy and Jo Shapcott, there are still preconceptions about poetry having to rhyme, act and perform in a certain way - it's rather like expecting a modern day schoolboy to doff his hat, play with a spinning top and run off down the street with a quarter of humbugs.

What role do you think poetry magazines and journals play in aiding eventual publication? Or do you think that pamphlets are becoming a more significant signpost?

Poetry magazines are vitally important. The best ones are like marvellous presents when they drop through the letterbox, because you know there will be new, judiciously chosen, luminous, and challenging material inside. You can practically hear the thoughts and words buzzing away inside the envelope like some bee that got trapped when it was stuck down. What amazes me more than anything (and without a hint of brown-nosing!) is the generosity of the editors. Bob Mee and Janet Murch, former Iota incumbents spent days sifting through mountains of submissions and molehills of subscriptions. No money is made and money is frequently lost in returning poems without the correct postage and so on. And yet without them, the transaction of contemporary poetry couldn't really happen. You may have thought with small audiences and high costs that the Internet is the simple answer, but it doesn't seem to have panned out like that. The Internet doesn't satisfy most poets' desire to 'get into print' and the page still has a much higher currency. The best magazines, however are cottoning on to the fact that readers and poets like a lively web presence as well - a place where readers can meet each other and share opinions about the latest issue. A magazine subscription base is also a community - with the magazine as its common interest. Pamphlets are also important - especially to get a sense of a poets wider body of work. There is still the problem of selling pamphlets of course, but coming to a reading armed with some will mean you are taken more seriously and have something to press into the palms of an impressed audience. It didn't happen to me this way, but pamphlets are increasingly seen as an established stepping stone to a full collection.

Could you tell me something about the themes and preoccupations in your writing and how they inform your work? And an ancillary question - which you may or may not wish to conflate with the first - would you say that your winning poem was similar to or diverges from these?

Most of my poems are small rebellions against the mundane. They are usually crammed with unusual detail - like a motorcyclist with a skeleton riding pillion behind her, or a photograph of Frank Sinatra stuck to the inside back window of a VW Beetle. It's usually stuff that I've observed and stuck into my notebook and saved for a rainy day - or at least until an idea to hang the poem on comes along. In the case of the motorcyclist, it became a rather macabre poem about a second honeymoon, a road trip featuring a woman and her late husband that ends with them both driving off the end of Southwold Pier. The usual preoccupations come up - death, love and religion, but I rarely tackle them head on - rather through an unusual story I've heard or imagined. Some poems are pure slights of fancy, like Norfolk is Heading out to Sea, in which the county breaks off from the rest of England and starts floating out towards Holland. Others are much closer to home - about a new born son, or rowing on an empty lake. These poems have a simplicity and honesty to them that can sometimes be just as engaging as the Technicolor narratives. I think Farewell to the Earth falls somewhere between the two, which is perhaps why it succeeds. It has a credible personal narrative, but is still laced with unusual material: the first line reads: 'We buried him with a potato in each hand.'

What was the initial impulse that kick started the writing of your winning poem?

I walked over to my friend Nick's house with my daughter one Saturday morning - the first visit of the new year. I knew his father was ill and naturally enough , asked 'how's your dad?' 'Dead', was the very short reply. After a moment's mortifying silence, we got chatting about the unusual circumstances of his funeral and about the fact that he had been a keen gardener. I was intrigued about the natural burial and the fact that they had dropped in some of his personal effects. Later that day, I jotted down some notes and wrote a draft of what I initially called 'Gardener's Farewell' within the week. I shared a copy with him and he was quite pleased - although of course I was a little nervous it was so soon after his loss. When I found out it had won, of course I let him know straight away. The family are actually quite touched and honoured. I should say at this point, the gardener's name was Paul Newman Keeble - dying in the same year as the other Paul Newman. I should also thank Nick for the being so candid and allowing the poem to be published.

With the proliferation at so many literature festivals of 'Celebrities' and some Poetry Festivals that seem to concentrate on 'The Tried and Tested' and 'Chosen By A Select Few' , I'd like to ask you about the 'politics' of readings. How difficult, or not, have you found it to access opportunities to read from your work? Considering all the hoops, in terms of timelines, representation, vetting – through peer review you have to go through?

I read sporadically at festivals, arts centres and pubs and I do generally enjoy giving performances of my work. I've mentioned that I've had invites on the back of competition wins as well as being in anthologies and magazines and whenever I can, I accept them. It's the single best way to sell copies of my book - people generally only buy a newcomer's work in the warm, fuzzy afterglow of a reading. I normally write a setlist and think about a little bit of patter to introduce the poems. Even if you give just a few establishing remarks, I find the audience much more likely to go with you. Otherwise, they're wondering what on earth the poem is about and trying to work out an appropriate response. Having said that, I find poetry audiences very finely tuned to mood and able to take on quite complex conceits and imagery - I suppose it helps that most people who listen are also poets, so there's usually an element of professional interest. To be honest, I haven't felt encumbered by any politics or felt like I've had to jump through any hoops. I once made the appalling error of reading a poem in a Northern Irish accent . . . not something to be repeated. Too often I trot out my 'greatest hits' - poems I know always go down well, but its much more rewarding reading something new. Time allowing, I'm always happy to accept an invitation to read or do a workshop.

Would you agree that it's essential for a poet to be heard as well as read, when you consider the tradition and its oral origins?

I wouldn't say it was essential - most people have a good aural imagination , but some peculiar magic happens when good poetry is read aloud. It's a reminder that poetry is rooted in sound; melody and rhythm. Whenever I write I always read what I've written aloud to make sure it's hanging together. It can read fine on the page, but translated in soundwaves can be leaden and flat. Most poetry 'from the tradition' was meant to be heard, remembered and repeated, which I suppose is why Gawain and Beowulf have distinctive alliteration patterns as well as thumping good narratives. Certainly four hours of Shakespeare's iambic lines in performance can do something to you it doesn't do on the page. The one thing I'm not into is declaiming or excessive formality. I was actually disappointed to hear an MP3 of MacNeice reading his work - his formal, clipped, dispassionate delivery seems at odds with the human sympathy and acute feeling in the work. And Robert Frost sounds like a dying king at the end of a dynasty - lighten up, you feel like saying - it's only a bit of snow! The best contemporary poets give naturalistic readings that somehow also project a confidence of purpose. You've got to sound convinced by your poem or it will drift into the air and vanish before your eyes. I'm one of those people who believe that bad poetry isn't poetry. I wish I could remember who said that?

Who are your major influences in writing and why? (It does not have to be poetry)

I started out reading Gerard Manley Hopkins and Elizabeth Jennings which reflected the tastes of my school English Teachers, and my early writing efforts were over complicated and quite classically 'undergraduate' -

everything was hyphenated! As I read wider, my poetry became simpler and clearer. At university I was exposed to all manner of things: Blake, Eliot, Harrison, the second world war poets, notably Alun Lewis and Keith Douglas whose stylish confidence really appealed to me. His line 'Shall I get drunk or cut myself a piece of cake,' struck me as a fabulous opener. (The cake reference I later found out referred to going with a prostitute, rather than a nice slice of Madeira). I enjoyed his painterly sensibility - using light as well as sound as an effect. I also enjoyed the American influence of Wallace Stevens, Frank O'Hara and Ginsberg. I enjoyed Ginsberg's late work where he wanders the midnight dime stores of New York unable to sleep, feeling old, irrascible and vaguely aroused. Of course, Heaney, Hughes, Armitage, Matthew Sweeney, Jo Shapcott, Jean Sprackland, W.N Herbert are all there in the background. I also liked Henry Shukman's book *In Dr No's Garden* and Betjeman is a bit of a guilty pleasure! My most recent discovery is a Scots poet called Alisdair Maclean who wrote comparatively little but whose collection *From the Wilderness* is a collection of dry, darkly comic and frequently surreal musings from the desolate crofts. It is very much in the vein of Hughes' 60's and 70's work. Outside poetry, I like a lot of Billy Bragg, Bruce Springsteen, Bob Dylan . . . anyone beginning with B, really. I'm also a huge admirer of the late environmental writer Roger Deacon. His two books *Waterlog* and *Wildwood* are always the ones I press into people's hands at the end of a dinner party. Which probably explains why I no longer have copies of his books in the house. I read less fiction, and I'm quite a slow reader, but would happily admit to enjoying D.H. Lawrence, Thomas Hardy, John Irving and Ian McEwan.

Interview by Alex McMillen

Farewell to the Earth

We buried him with a potato in each hand
on New Year's Day when the ground was hard as luck,
wearing just cotton, his dancing shoes plus
a half bottle of pear cider to stave off the thirst.

In his breast pocket we left a taxi number
and a packet of sunflower seeds; at his feet was
the cricket bat he used to notch up a century
against the Fenstanton eleven.

We dropped in his trowel and a shower of rosettes
then let the lid fall on his willow casket.
The sky was hard as enamel; there was
a callus of frost on the face of the fields.

Dust to dust; but this was no ordinary muck.
The burial plot was by his allotment, where
the water butt brimmed with algae and the shed door
swung and slammed as we shook back the soil.

During the service, my mother asked
the funeral director to leave; take away some hair
and the resemblance was too close; and yet
my father never looked so smart.

I kept expecting him to walk in, his brow
steaming with rain, soil under his fingernails,
smelling of hot ashes and compost;
looking for fresh tea in the pot.

Returning

We return in the dark like cat burgulars
swallowing the echo of our own footsteps.
Green jewels blink on the garden wall.
The night is enlarged by a single click of the lock.
With shoulder bags, duvets, our babies
pressed to our sides, the front door resists us:
the spindrift of letters and bills, postcards
pushed aside like the collective hush
of paperbacks in a midnight passenger lounge.
Our babies are limp in our arms, flour sacks
we drop into their own unfamiliar beds.

Three weeks of silence have collected here;
nothing but the claptrap of the letterbox
once a day, and the weekly stuffing of the free paper.
Dust has coated the rooms in strangeness.
Time has trapped itself in our house.
Light switches have edged an inch along each wall.
I bundle out the last of the bags and click the keyfob:
the double indicator flash as I lock the car.
Across the road, I see a curtain twitch.
The Victorians are asleep in their beds;
their children are at the window watching us.

Versology

I started out like all the rest - in the bedroom
with a couple of decks, a Hawaiian shirt, a pair of headphones
and the collected works of Wallace Stevens.
I bleached my hair, practiced my sestinas
and tried mixing Bukowski with Emily Bronte.
There were some early failures.
I trawled the sound archives, loaded up
some Frost on the ipod and remixed some Armitage.
By this time, I was playing parties for free
warming them up with a sonnet or two
before unleashing some Fenton; I put Howl on a loop
and made moonlight of their minds.
When I hit the clubs I was already a name
spinning Past Lives Therapy and Ezra Pound;
I played T.S.Eliot at the Ministry of Sound.
Most of them were out of it, coming up
on Gary Snyder, whispering lines
of Migration of Birds in the washrooms.
Girls with flushed cheeks passed me their numbers
high on Plath and with grins as wide as Hungarian clowns.
At the bar they'd barely sell a drink all night.
Afterwards, we'd meet up in midnight cafes
spark up some Muldoon and wait for the buzzing to stop.
We'd swipe the new Sweeney from each other's laptops.
By the time I played Brighton Beach
a quarter of a million showed up, calling for Ginsburg
in one voice; I fooled them with a verse of Kaddish
then played Ted Hughes reading from Crow.
The air shook like an earthquake inside a mountain.
That night the moon was like honey; the sea
as calm as Elizabeth Bishop's Club Classics Volume 3.

Christopher James

Second Honeymoon

She headed east,
on his gleaming Norton 500,
his skeleton riding pillion.
The cooling towers sprung
like mushrooms on the flat horizon.

She slaked her thirst on fen-water
and Suffolk ale while the wind
blew through his bones.

The first night, they camped
In Walberswick and blasted out
American Beauty on the stereo;
She lit a joint and let the blue smoke
drift in one ear and out the other.

At Southwold she pulled up outside
the Swan Hotel and paid cash for two
white roses and a glass of champagne.

Unchallenged, she soft peddled
onto the pier, weaved the handlebars
through the arcade then hit the gas.

With a final gasp, she cleared the railing
leaving just a ninepin of floating bones,
her purple scarf and a note which read:
Please remember to feed my cat.

From *The Invention of Butterfly* (Ragged Raven) 2006

Iota Submissions

Poetry

Iota magazine welcomes submissions of new poetry. Please send no more than six poems. We do not accept simultaneous submissions or previously published work. Poems must be in English, the original work of the author and translations must be marked as such, with the title and the author of the original poem included. Submissions are judged anonymously so your name should not appear on the poetry. Include a separate sheet with your name, address and a full list of poems submitted. No email submissions will be accepted. We will reply within three months. The decision of the Editorial Board is final.

Fiction

The Iota fiction and prose edition welcomes submissions of short fiction and non-fiction for consideration. Short stories and other pieces should be between 2000 and 6000 words and must be the original work of the author. We accept translations as long as they are indentified as such. All work must be typed and double spaced. We accept electronic submissions and all posted work will be returned provided the appropriate return postage is provided. Our aim is to respond within four months. Please send concise proposals for features. We also accept new fiction for review and correspondence to the Editor. Please email submissions, proposals and correspondence to *fiction@iotamagazine.co.uk*

Subscriptions

Single Issue: £6.50 UK
£8 Overseas

Three Issues: £15 UK
£25 Overseas

Ten Issues: £40 UK
£60 Overseas

Institutional Rate: £50 UK
£70 Overseas per annum
(three copies of each issue)

Lifetime subscription*: £200 UK
£250 Overseas

Iota Subscriptions
PO BOX 7721
Matlock
DE4 9DD
UK

*for as long as the magazine is published

Also available online from our website
www.iotamagazine.co.uk

Reviews

The Broken Word by Adam Foulds
Cape £9.00

Set in 1950s Kenya, in the midst of the Mau
Mau uprising, this novella in verse approaches
the period that marked the end of British
colonial rule, from the perspective of Tom.
Returning from school to his family farmstead
for the summer before leaving for university
in Britain we follow this unsympathetic yet
fascinating character as he plays his part in the
atrocities. We are led through his time serving
as a prison guard, in what has been described
as 'Britain's Gulag' into which the majority
of the Kikuyu population were driven. The
journey ends in Oxford where, although
thousands of miles away from Kenya, Foulds
demonstrates that the legacy of such activity
and experience is almost viral and certainly
timeless.

We begin travelling on a train that takes
us to Tom's home. There in '3: Dinner (2)'
Foulds lays out the environment of servitude
that was established in the period with
succinctness.

A senior houseboy served the soup.
They skimmed their spoons Correctly,
without noise, not touching china.

The dinner conversation develops an ominous
tone:

...I hazarded a hundred,
plus household staff.

I don't think we need to worry about them.

Jenkins laughed, dabbing up soup.
I would start with them.

Foulds' choice of layout represents
conversation effectively and the clear space
between lines along with the uncomplicated
brevity of their meaning gave me the feeling
I was eavesdropping, achieving a sense of
dramatic tension that is increased here with
the heightened yet sparse:

And I hope you all know how to shoot.

The speed with which the 'action'
unfolds from herein is swift, both in terms
of the colonial response to the uprising and
in relation to the adult world into which
our protagonist is thrust. After a brief
introduction to the men who make up the
Home Guard, Tom is dispatched into the world
by his father.

But you should go, Tom.
You'll be useful . And it's time,
I'm afraid, you know,
to be a man and all that.

Having already witnessed the slain corpses
of loyalist elders Tom takes part in a hunt of
retribution, first reluctantly as a bystander and
eventually, instinctively.

...Tom shot him.
Just like in a Western...
Only the fall backwards was different,
looser and ugly, spastic, almost embarrassing.

The stark way in which Foulds 'reports'
what Tom witnesses is both consistent and
heightened by the banal. We continue to
follow Tom as he works in a prison camp.

Sores growing on the prisoners like coral.
Buckets. Drills. Beatings. Boredom.

Foulds never describes anything like regret or ethical dilemma within Tom, and indeed, it seems he is not mature enough to encounter such. Instead, we observe the physical, the tangible.

The flies landed on you
...to eat the dead skin, dirt, lay their eggs
in the nutritious wetness of wounds.

As his admiration for the guards around him increases, Tom is inevitably drawn to emulate their violence, and the final section at the camp ends with Tom shooting a prisoner in a mixture of whim and hysteria.

His return home is swift and his communication with his parents is limited to the socially correct. In an atmosphere where talking openly about the reality of events is impossible Tom is faced with his parents' disappointment.

Tom, I don't want you living
with the shame of crying off
of something difficult for the rest of your life.

At university Tom is unable to wash-along with the rest of the student flotsam and appears to struggle with carrying the weight of his experiences silently. However, his recently established brutality seeps out in the company of a love interest, first, in the proximity of a bar brawl, and then sexually in what the reader expects will be the end of his romance.

Foulds leaves the reader with a definite point of departure when Tom is told:

young men start looking,
you know, do I have to
spell it out? In jewellers' windows.

This positioning of the future is both sobering and eerie. Again, Foulds incorporates the mundane, this time middle class expectation, with the inference of the lifelong impact that Tom's experience will have on those he shares his future with.

This was a collection that was both hard and easy to read. In terms of pace and structure it felt a breeze but in terms of the subject matter it made me feel terribly alone with knowledge. This, I think, is the collection's strength and it doesn't surprise me that Foulds was recently named the Sunday Times Young Writer of the Year.

Kate North

The Lamplighter
Jackie Kay
Bloodaxe £9.95

Jackie Kay's dramatic poem was written to commemorate the 200th anniversary of the abolition of the slave trade. As the author wrote in the Guardian, she was initially reluctant to take the commission:

...I thought that enough had been written about slavery, and that I didn't want to be pigeonholed as a black writer...

Research into the subject helped change her mind and she used testimonies and original accounts to shape her work. The collection comes with an accompanying CD of the BBC radio recording of the text that has been much praised. The story is delivered with five voices, one male and four female, and details experiences in the slave fort, the ship, the plantations and of the impact this economic process had on the British industrial revolution.

The narrative focuses on the lives of four women, Constance, Mary, Harriot and the Lamplighter. Through these characters Kay tells of forced separation, loss, violence, sexual exploitation, resistance, survival and the job memory plays in keeping such experiences present.

Kay places much emphasis on the sensory as with these lines:

We sweated and dripped continually…

I could hear the sugarbirds whistling…

Till my fingers looked like bindweed

This serves to locate the historical in the realm of the personal. Such details allow the text to speak to a contemporary audience in an intimate manner. In turn, I felt as though the characters worked to speak with the voices of the countless unheard and that the telling was in itself of primary import.

In taking this course Kay does not negate the inherent complications and contradictions that arise when approaching such an expansive history. Oftentimes the characters' voices are crystalised in this confusion:

Mary:
    I tell my story to remember.

Black Harriot:
    I tell my story to forget.

As a result the reader is forced to confront the necessity of remembering along with the pain of doing so. Thematically, the presence of absence roars through the work and Kay is adept at ensuring we never forget the very physical repercussions of events that are often supposed to have dissolved with time.

Mary:
    There is not a brick in this city

Lamplighter:
    But what is cemented with the blood of a
slave

Constance (sings):
    Bristol belongs to me.

This history is something that concerns us all in the present and the Lamplighter is a strong acknowledgment of this. I feel that such a work would be well placed on the secondary curriculum to ensure that this

frequently silent history is subject to the process of re-memory that it clearly deserves.

Kate North

Farewell My Lovely
Polly Clark
Bloodaxe £7.95

Farewell My Lovely does contain a number of great poems (the title poem being an obvious standout); but by far the strongest voice within this collection is that found in the final section of this book.

'I Thought It Was in Scotland' is a sparse series of seven poems, written in the voice of a seventeen year old soldier serving in the Falklands. The intensity of voice, the intonation of innocence and the crush of reality are palpable in every one; 'Dear Mum' was not only exceptional in terms of (re) constructing form, but its honest and brutal representation of the internal conflict of its narrator left me close to tears. Clark cleverly interweaves the epistolary narrative between what this soldier tells his mother and the reality of what he is actually experiencing. She achieves this by scoring through the unsavoury narrative – whilst this technique isn't new – it is employed with exceptional effect.

~~Mummy his brain~~
~~Came out on my hands~~

Serg says we'll be home by my birthday!
Funny that I can fight a war but can't drink!

Hard to write cos it's very noisy!
~~Mummy I don't think you'll know me~~

~~I tried to hold his head together~~
~~I said it would be all right~~

There are other aspects to praise within this collection; in the title poem, her capacity for unexpected imagery and devastating simile is often exquisite;

...

the sea with a face I'd like to smack,
the loosening sky, fit to drop —

as I'm dusting the mirror
I glimpse her, smart as a rat
in the company of rocks —

If there is any aspect of this collection I am disappointed with, it is Clarke's tendency to be a little too sentimental (which is in stark contrast to the latter section of the book); in 'Return to Eden' and 'Advice to a Daughter' particularly, the tone is too conversational, too generic to achieve any intensity of a genuine voice. However, there are enough strong poems in this collection to counterbalance those that don't quite stand up to scrutiny.

In conclusion, when I reached the end of the collection, I felt a little cheated; 'I Thought It Was in Scotland' seemed tacked on, which both saddened and surprised me – I am not a renowned fan of war poetry (of any era) – and yet I couldn't help but feel there was a bigger story to be told through this voice, more than any other within the book, if Polly Clarke ever writes that story - I'd buy the collection tomorrow.

Sonia Hendy-Isaac

A Knowable World
Sarah Wardle
Bloodaxe £7.95

This autobiographical collection promised something of the unspoken, a viewpoint rarely written; that of the bipolar self within the constraints of the mental health system. For the author to write such a book, no doubt took courage, but the result is, ultimately, somewhat mixed.

With such an intriguing subject matter, I had expected poetry that would offer me a new insight into the frustrations experienced within bipolar episodes. Whilst there are moments that attempt to tease these emotions out, such as 'Exchange', in which the notions of the reflected and fractured self are interwoven, it feels that the author is somehow holding back – the metaphor is under worked and the result is a poem that only offers us a recollection and not a revelation.

Wardle has a passion for end-rhyme, this is not in itself a crime, but the effect of this constant trope makes me question her word choice; for example in 'Semantics of Psychiatry', 'fathom' is rhymed with 'bunkum' - is this the best word or simply there to satisfy the (half)rhyme? In the opening poem, 'Magnetic Resonance Imaging', the a,b,a,b rhyme scheme distracts somewhat from the potential intensity of the poem;

Then for an hour loud sounds crashed and banged,
as I lay in this nuclear missile
of clinical white and my brain was scanned
for shading of schizophrenic detail.

The use of lazy phrases, such as 'sounds crashed and banged', adds little to force the reader on; although admittedly the tension found on the next line fosters a more interesting image.

There is also a tendency for poetic ticks; whilst Wardle's understandable conflict with authority is, no doubt, relevant to her experience, its repetition is found in no fewer than eight of the poems. There are also a clutch of four/five line poems which add little by way of interest or depth to the collection. But by far, the most obtrusive tick was the use of beginning and end: 'a starting to an end' (Turquoise), 'the beginning of ending' (Found Audience) and 'a beginning of ending' (Sarah, wife of Abraham). I am sure that others may argue a case for 'trope' rather than tick – but because these poems are positioned together in a seven page space, it forced me to question whether there might be a more intriguing way to show this sense of collapse.

Sonia Hendy-Isaac

Etymology
Bryan Walpert
Cinnamon Press £7.99

As the title indicates, Walpert's thematic intention is to explore the roots of language, definitions and meanings, which he does. Etymology can be fascinating – I welcome every opportunity to expand my understanding of a word; however the key to exploring the etymology within poetry is surely (as Pound would state) to make it new. In 'Ugly', Walpert cleverly juxtaposes his etymological intentions with an exploration of a relationship and the upbringing of the couple within that relationship, which in and of itself represents attention to craft. However, my patience was somewhat exhausted by no less than four definitions of the word 'ugly' and its respective connectives. However in the closing lines, Walpert demonstrates the potential power of his rhetoric – when he allows the abstract to collide with the physical, the effect is exhilarating:

'the former
with a taste like truth, the latter
sweet as ignorance, sticky like childhood.'

Certainly the stronger poems in this collection were those that contained nothing more than a nod towards the meaning of a word rather than its roots; in 'Late', he offers an intimate, sensual and fiercely considered snapshot of the first love of a late bloomer, but even in this exceptional poem I found an issue of breath in his composition:

'I left my first job each night with a film
of cooking grease on my skin, my hair, soaked
into the brown corduroys and the dancing carrots
and cauliflowers printed on the shirt

they made us wear in July,'

Throughout the collection there is a tendency for long lines. However, if you follow the punctuation on the page, his use of enjambment means that some lines are difficult to read aloud. The other issue that occasionally threw me out of his poems were the line breaks; maybe Walpert is of the opinion that each line needn't hold itself as an individual unit of sense, and that weak line endings are a matter of choice; but frankly it distracted me unnecessarily, especially in the opening poem 'No Metaphor':

'the weight on his back less like

a broken-hearted lament than a bulky
instrument. This sight, it's true, might
remind someone less sensible than you
of a duet, of a girl, of the year'

Aside from 'broken-hearted', there are too many lines which don't hold as units of sense in the poem. I could perhaps overlook this if this only occurred once or twice, but there are just too many poems where this occurs in the collection.

In conclusion, there are aspects of this collection that I really enjoyed, his imagery is often incredibly strong, and his invocation of the senses, is at times, faultless. Sadly, I was left with the feeling that the overriding theme of the collection, all too often, overrode his strengths.

Sonia Hendy-Isaac

A Twist of Malice: uncomfortable poems by older women
Joy Howard (ed.)
Grey Hen Press, £8.00
Bundle o'Tinder
Rose Kelleher
The Waywiser Press, £7.99

Do you prefer anthologies or collections? I owe my long acquaintance with many favourite poets to school anthologies. (I wish more anthologies appeared on current syllabuses.)

Anthologies are gateways: the only poetry books, if any, present in many households. As long as good poems flare within their pages, my one reservation, as a writer, about the current best-sellers is that I would love more of my own work smuggled into them. But, as a reader, I must admit that as soon as I find an interesting anthologised poem, I long to flee the anthology for the coherence and intensity of one of the poet's collections.

I must dispel the smoke of unsuitability by stressing that although I may not be the keenest reader of anthologies, I am sympathetic to this anthology's chosen twists. In my careless twenties, I did not believe that women faced any particular obstacles to publishing poetry. I now know that they may face particular difficulties in writing it, sometimes through the workings of family, where problems may spring from either sex. Clearly there are some very fine, and moving poems now available for publication from older women, which compete for oxygen with accomplished material from much younger writers.

I admire the boldness of the editor of 'A Twist of Malice'. She declares 'First and foremost, this anthology is meant to entertain'. A wicked smile adorns the cover. How do you write entertainingly about malice? Perhaps by a patient powder-trail of detail, such as Jude Goodwin's 'smoky rose/ dress' or Ann Alexander's menus, 'She will have latte, sponge fingers'- en route to a killer ending:

> Of course I didn't gloat
> I never say a thing.'
>
> (Berta Freistadt)

> 'They will be leaving early.
> I will be picking up the bill.
>
> (Ann Alexander)

Ingenuity helps to delay the explosion. Alice Beer's vengeful first wife in 'Time Out', who will 'slip in just before one' to the place she is 'staying', is, in fact, dead. M R Peacocke's brevity echoes on after the mysterious voice caught in an orchard: 'My spade/ struck on stone/ No one.'

A surprising absence in this anthology, of the echoes of history, is highlit by Pamela Coren's sudden reference to 'the arrow-slit where the barons shot my father'. But Ann Alexander brings a stylish reworking of Snow White: 'God knows I tried [...] I took a course in parenting. She cried.' Angela France catches the lilt of myth: 'She returns from the sea with a boy child', who 'salts his drink of water'.

Salt in the flame may cast a benevolent light. Ann Drysdale's Eve drinks, in lazy couplets,

Out in the garden in a dressing gown
Breathing old apples as the sun goes down.

But the poems' shocks darken, far beyond the entertainment of light verse. Clare Shaw's poem is a troubling child 'its spiteful little elbows in my back'. Ruth Silcock's incantatory 'Perils of Ageing' throws the old to the wolves. Marianne Burton's roses eat the dead:

the firm ones, the green ones, the liquid ones.

Gil McEvoy's language, for all its passing pleasures, is forged under the pressure of pain, the weight of a life:

For I'm a hard woman now:
I am diamond, carborundum,
and I wipe out fools.

Two hard judgements could be made upon this book. Its slightly confused subject headings do not illuminate the poems. It is rather too indulgent to writers who favour feeling over form. Anne Stewart, whose Christmas poem ends in the sly rhyme 'hatchet', shows that elegance may be a good friend to malice.

Yet 'A Twist of Malice' is also a good friend to its reader. Its editor boldly allocates generous space to each poet. This risks repetition, and alienation of an unsympathetic reader, but it can also allow the poems of a previously unknown poet to explode and flower in the mind. I was increasingly mesmerised by the dark powers of Ruth Sharman. I would not like to be left alone with her scrambling vines, her choking waterlilies, or the quiet 'white garden' which she turns into a jungle. Nor would I open her wardrobe:

The dress

he hooked me into was my wedding dress,
and it was black and fitted like a skin.

But the skilfully twisted fuse of this anthology will light my path to her full collection.

I must turn to another collection, Rose Kelleher's 'Bundle o' Tinder'. This book won the Anthony Hecht Poetry Prize for 2007. Richard Wilbur has contributed a foreword of glowing praise. I can only agree, humbly. This first collection is a revelation. Here is the ending of the first poem, 'Asperger's Muse', about a boy who chants numbers, remembered and reproduced by Kelleher:

71693993;
Seeking spoken sanctuary
in the perfect circle's key
he draws a closed perimeter
around himself; and though I cannot
understand the tongue he speaks,
I know he sings a hymn to something
steady, central, infinite.

The short, delicately rhymed lines settle into a hypnotic, falling rhythm, like a Shakespearian charm. Kelleher's own reverent listening entrances the reader. This is the slow fuse of poetry, from patient technical tricks to vision.

'Asperger's Muse' opens into celebration, but Kelleher's poems frequently close with hint and menace. A quiet list of the features of a school ends with 'the rectangle' (also the poem's title) 'where Father Geoghan's portrait used to hang'. In 'Famine Ship', the memory of a slaver begins to unfold, also in a tense final line:

the freight we carried twenty years ago.

The poem has done its work. The line sinks into the reader's mind, igniting echo and story. One of Kelleher's strengths is her remarkable ability to confront two worlds, as in 'Not Our Dog', the story of an adoption:

and the dog

growls low in its throat, and bares its teeth at me
while I choose curtains for the nursery.

Kelleher's is a tough, colloquial voice. Her outspoken poem 'Lourdes' addresses the sacred place as a fallible person: 'You're hard to get to/ and can't fix everything'. But she is not afraid, finally, to expose her own desire: 'Cure my doubt.' Kelleher's short lines are excellent, an unshowy proof of strength.

My praise for Kelleher acquired a colleague for this review. My husband, sceptical about the worth of much new poetry, read the whole of 'Bundle o' Tinder', captivated by its humour and by the delicate, playful sensuousness of 'How Ticklishness Evolved':

whose touch was feather-soft before it stung.

I was particularly moved by 'Neanderthal Bone Flute', which shows a rather different Kelleher, eloquent and bare. Her work does not depend upon lush adjectives but upon an inner vision overflowing into sound, as the syllables at this poem's close overflow the measure of the traditional sonnet:

Let bone be flute, the music in our marrow.

The poem is its own music, but in hoping that the Neanderthal musician might be our ancestor, Kelleher, as she admits, defies the taut subject heading for this poem, 'Science'. Yet she is often adept at integrating science into her poetry and her vision. 'Impulse' refers to synapse and robot before - without contradiction - 'The spirit moves'.

It is a bold ending. Kelleher's diction also often startles. A giant ray's landing is 'the splat'. This is accuracy, not conceit. Though she can deploy rhetoric most effectively, Kelleher is never histrionic. The final lines of a short poem about September 11 are charged by understatement:

preferring to go on just as before
but loving what I loved a little more.

I have few reservations about 'Bundle o' Tinder'. Occasionally a theme is stretched too thinly – although across very well-made bones – as in the various mermaids and crabs in 'At Sea'. Very occasionally a poem struck me as rather crowded and overwrought. The frantic lists of 'Gingernut' end by stretching word order to the limit. The fuse can snap:

            nor is the fox
with its slim black feet more elegantly dressed.

Yet, two pages on, how eloquently Kelleher summarises the great 'Rays at Cape Hatteras', as they rise briefly above the sea: 'rude fliers in the face of disbelief'.

I stand in awe of Kelleher's formal accomplishment. Technique is the imagination's fuse. This book's strength is underpinned by varied quatrains, three-line stanzas, passionate sonnets and quick couplets. Its rhythms include falling trochaics, quietly authoritative iambic pentameters and the often despised, essential, lilt of folksong. Rhymes in multi-syllable words often sound facetious in English, but Kelleher's delicate use of part-rhymes is both serious and spirited:

be you saint or Aztec goddess
heal the earth, cast out the darkness.
Evil times are now upon us.

One of her favourite stanzas is the brooding quatrain, abba. This is a reflective collection, whose brief title is not explained until the heart of her book, in 'Ditty'. 'The saddest songs are those that burn/ black as a match and a bundle o'tinder.' Kelleher commands, 'Slowly unroll each note,'

I would note that there is not a bad poem in this book. Page after page delivers excellence, a memorable line, a jolt to the heart. Why was 'Bundle o' Tinder' not on every English prize list? Perhaps this is a slow-burning poetry. Collections blaze; but the anthologist may be the more patient incendiary.

Alison Brackenbury

The Fossil-Box
Richard Marggraf Turley
Cinnamon Press £7.99

In his first collection, Richard Marggraf Turley works through the most affective confessionality in the most refreshing of form. Just like the Romantics writing on nature to covertly continue with a proliferation of radical, political ideal, here, Marggraf Turley skilfully employs nature to document the sometimes political movement of the self coming together in view of an environment; nature as language.

I come to myself

                    (Little Dean, 2)

The collection is a mine of intense introspection, the lyric 'I' in reconciliation with landscapes of the past: The Forest of Dean and the Ceredigion coast. The present selfhood is knitted into a Wordsworthian re-examination of the formative environment, the necessity of returning to a locus of origin, the implication of the first person singular.

Not sure where I stand.
I've avoided it for years.
Redshifting from the forest,
delayed by my own momentum,

a boy seeing forms and faces
in the trees, I cast my eye
up to the hanging questions
that could be bats.

(Blackeney, 8)

Marggraf Turley does not have experimental or deconstructive agendas, but he does highlight the uncanny tensions between the world, our perception and re-presentation of it in language. A collection-long concentration of sight images, the use of the eye as 'I', performs an uncertain encounter with the world, manifest in the reflection of language and memory. The eye/I is overburdened in a rich chainmail of syntax, a stream of monosyllables. There is sensory excess in 'hanging questions' and 'borderless worlds', (Stars) heterogeneous masses that the eye/I must itself be part of.

No name for the hewn scowles
we dared not enter, bare rents
of rock thatched with ferric
yew, drawn to the iron.

(Blakeney, 4)

The result is secular and existential; a scaling of the self into the landscape, the magnitude of the setting and its intricacies barely broken down by the eye/I, which is left to run nomadic through nature and language. Each time the eye/I is evoked, its presence is alien and alone, an itinerant metalanguage skimming the environment as sight or self.

Marggraf Turley aligns the 'I' of the present with the diverse backdrop of natural past by way of answering his own prayer:

Give me the wisdom to wield
power over words.

His linguistic agility closes, rather than opens the gap between the self and the surrounding. Language is made malleable, breaching an almost ineffable degree of referential precision. His 'Faceted eyes' acknowledge all the hidden depths in ourselves

and in our world.

Afterwards, you un-
fold, sit drying
your wings, watching
the pupated world

with faceted eyes.

The musicality of the collection has attracted critical acclaim, the intensity and authenticity of the vocabulary is undeniably striking. However, the detectable connection to the Romantic sometimes stifles Marggraf Turley's own voice; there is emphatic attachment to archaic resonances, such as 'caught my fancy', and '(what) do I owe these vales?' Still, The Fossil-Box is visually enticing, with an excellent experiment in harsh enjambment:

puzzle-	*con-*	*imp-*
work	*glomerate*	*ression*

The splitting of well chosen words extracts a pulpy centre of differential meaning, more apparent when read aloud. A well-anticipated CD version of this outstanding first collection follows shortly. Richard Marggraf Turley's new collection, *Wan-Hu's Flying Chair* is out later this month.

Lucy Tyler

Sea Change
Jorie Graham
Carcanet £9.95

Since her 1996 Pulitzer Prize winning *The Dream of the Unified Field*, what we have come to expect from Graham's poetry is an exposure of actuality: an absorbing amalgamation of important global issues, embedded in stark formal innovation.

This eleventh collection is no exception.

The site of *Sea Change* is the illusive borderland of present and future. A nightmare place where climate change is more than imminent, it is in progress.

My Species is ill
         (The Violinist at the Window, 1918)

The first thing you will notice is Graham's approach to her theme. These poems follow an enduring form: a collection-long, peripatetic legato to staccato movement, overlaid with a post-symbolist usage of metaphor.

This is a collection of love poems; the natural world is the speaker's object of desire, and each poem, a love letter to one aspect of the environment:

'Midwinter.', 'Full moon.', 'After great rain.' and 'Summer heat.' etc.

The poems are schematized similarly: how does she love the Midwinter? Graham counts the ways. A poem unfolds itself prosaically; it fondles every detail of the love object: *the cuttlefish branches, the cloud on blue ground, the blur of spear roots.*

                             (Futures)

The page brims with sensory expression 'everything unpreventable and excited' is manifest in a uproar of colour and rhythmic buoyancy. A fresh vision of Romantic imagery runs uninterruptedly over several sentences.

...running towards me. Then here you
        are, you came all this
            distance,

                             (Loan)

The geometry of line breaking is important here. The reader is acclimatised to a largo, somnambulistic movement around an image of nature, which without notice, procreates insistent velocity. A sweep forward, and the relationship between speaker and love object reaches a dead end.

& what
     says the eye-thinking heart,   *is the*
            last colour seen, the last word
heard
                    (Futures)

Graham's form enacts the art of human destruction upon the images of nature.

The syntagmatic necessity, the driving progression that the form inspires, suddenly stunts, shuts down on, and squishes the epicentral image.

As readers, we are never allowed to recoil from this uncanny moment; the 'tipping point' of loss, which Graham's trademark enjambment generates. It serves as a painful reminder that humanity has arrived at the finale of its comfort zone.

Line breaks take control. Like humanity, form doesn't notice its own destructive paradigm. The emphatic interest in the beloved image of nature, is sullied in its drag. The reality of environmental crisis becomes manifest.

An image is pushed to the precipice. The reader is dropped off, left teetering on the claustrophobic right hand side of the page. We start in present, comfortable prosody. We finish in the future with nothing.

Neither nature, nor the present can be sustained; we take both for granted. We forget that they are fallible, and will collapse, wilt and degenerate.

In the frightening poem, 'Root End', Graham engenders this atmosphere of devastation better than anywhere else. In the line breaks, every image undergoes a violent disappearing act, subsumed in mortality; it expires, and is forgotten.

             the dusk is already
crushed tight and cannot be looked into/ anymore

The music of Graham's form provokes change in its terrifying jolt of white space and line break, which emulates natural disaster. Graham lays bare the chaos of what it would be like to see everything we hold dear, ruined.

The form of *Sea Change* is so self-destructive, that it forces the language into rhetorical questioning.

.... who shall repair this now. And how the future
  takes shape
  too quickly. The permanent is ebbing. Is leaving
nothing....

A semi-philosophical, metaphysical volta always sidesteps the initial natural image. The focus of the work is deliberately blurred, cascaded over strands of language, and out of the blue, before you know it, Graham has moved on; the self-centred human speaker cuckolds the love object of nature.

Midwinter. Dead of. I own you says my mind.
  Own what?

(Futures)

A colloquial liveliness separates sites of divergent modulation and lexicon. Like line breaks, they contribute to a sense of disruption; the poems are not about what we think they are about, but about the process that the form inspires. The visual trajectory seems to follow an overarching chronology; the reader is forced to acknowledge that change is at constant groundswell, and could upsurge at any moment.

It is not necessary to read Graham's interviews to realise that *Sea Change* is not intended as categorically polemical, an advocation of global issues. If it were, poetry would seem a limited tool for dissemination. As Graham has stated previously, she wants *Sea Change* to 'serve art foremost', to attract consideration only as poetry, relaying a Keats-esque consideration of the transition of beauty.

Form establishes itself as organic matter, an ivy, thriving and enveloping, then hacked down and dissected, added to, then taken away from. It is beautiful then disfigured, disfigured then beautiful. In this way, Graham makes the destructive process natural and inevitable. Perhaps she is being provocative, forcing us to accept environmental loss as certainty.

Numbered rows grew / numberless long / ago.

(Root End)

It is hard to believe therefore, that Graham does not see herself as educative; an Al Gore type, establishing more inconvenient truth. Her writing echoes with prophecy, an anxious glance of future, the pending and irreversible global destruction. Poems like 'Underworld' carry Old Testament credence; the punishable forces of the natural world unite.

My god gave
it me says the evaporation sluicing invisible
  surfaces

Whether or not she has meant to, Graham's collection decides publicly the artist has an educative role, a social responsibility to document current affairs and matters of universal importance. *Sea Change* relates a terrifying sense of imminent human catastrophe, a disparaging prompt, an extended farewell to our loves, our ideological strongholds and any sense of infallibility.

Although this poetry collection is exceptional and important, surely it must be important for poets to consider themselves free, rather than socially obligated to educate. If Graham has done both, then that can only be excellent.

Lucy Tyler

An Leabhar Mòr: The Great Book of Gaelic
Malcom MacLean & Theo Dorgan (eds.)
O'Brien Press, £39.99

O'Brien Press is to be congratulated on the production of such a beautiful book. It really is a pleasure to see the highest production standards being applied unstintingly. This is a reprint of a book first published in Great Britain by Cannongate in 2002. The book is well served by several good introductions from Malcolm MacLean, Duncan MacMillan, Colm

Ó Baoill, Ronald Black and Theo Dorgan, who between them cover ancient and modern Irish and Scottish Gaelic poetry and visual art. The main body of the book is given over to presentation of the poems, or more exactly in many cases, excerpts of the poems, translations on the left hand page and accompanying visual art on the right hand page. The artworks have been carefully chosen so that they are either directly influenced by the poem they stand in juxtaposition with, or they share some common aspect of influence.

The book contains a broad sweep of the best poems in Irish and Scottish Gaelic from the anonymous texts of the 6th – 9th centuries, the high poets of the Gaelic courts and poems of patronage, the wandering bards of the 18th century, the poets of the early to mid 20th century and contemporary poets. In terms of volume, the skew is towards the more modern work, perhaps not unsurprisingly given the method of nomination used, where fifteen contemporary poets from each territory had one poem each included and were asked to nominate two others. However, this is one of the strengths of the book. It allows a generous and broad taste of what is being written now and what has been written recently, but also places that work within the wider linguistic tradition that influenced it.

This book will serve as a good introduction to the long and valuable tradition of Gaelic poetry while also demonstrating the vibrancy of the new and recent writing. On the Irish side, many familiar poems present themselves 'Dubh' by Nuala Ní Dhomnaill, for instance, her great poem on the fall of Srebrenica, which only really works in Irish, using as it does the sound of the word 'dubh' (black) to imitate the whizzing of bullets throughout the piece. Gearóid MacLochlainn is represented, but I really wish 'Teanga' had been used, with its pulsing rhythms reminiscent of rap. MacLochlainn is one of the most exciting and experimental of the new Irish poets and it would have been good to bring that out more. I wondered also if there was an opportunity to add a poet or two who had emerged since the first edition of 2002. Perhaps an opportunity has been missed there. Incidentally, one notes that Biddy Jenkinson's work is accompanied by a verse translation. Jenkinson has long refused to have her work translated in print in Ireland and one wonders if this shows some relaxing of that position or whether it is an accidental result of reprinting a book originally published in Great Britain.

I found much to admire in the new Scottish Gaelic writers also, although I must confess that I was ignorant of many of them up to now. Anna C. Frater whose work is new to me struck me with her rhythmic lyricism and Rody Gorman whose work I did know, and some of whose poems I have translated in the past, is represented by an experimental macaronic. If these poets are representative of the breadth and range of that generation, then poetry in Scottish Gaelic is a healthy as its Irish counterpart.

My quibbles with the book amount to minor annoyance at the necessity of relegating sections of the work (sometimes more than half the poem) to an appendix. I can see why it was done, but surely a more sensible strategy might have been to present the Gaelic on the page facing the artwork and relegate the translation to the appendix if necessary. The other quibble is what appears to be an uncharacteristic slip in Theo Dorgan's Introduction regarding Micheál Ó hAirtnéide and Caitlín Maude, who he says 'carry the mid-century'. Surely his timeline is a little off here, since both of those published their debut collections in 1975. If we consider that the mid-century was punctuated by debut collections by Máirtin Ó Direáin (Coinnle Geala, 1942), Seán Ó Ríordáin (Eireaball Spideoige, 1952), Máire Mhac an tSaoi (Margadh na Saoire, 1956) and Seán Ó Tuama (Faoileán na Beatha, 1961). Perhaps these poets (even Ó Tuama is a stretch) might be more worthy of that description.

These minor criticisms aside, I think it's a valuable and gorgeous book and I wish its re-issue every success.

Nigel McLoughlin

Time Gentlemen Please
Kevin Higgins
Salmon Poetry €12.00

Kevin Higgins' second collection follows on from the success of his first with more striking, surprising and cuttingly observed work. To take an example from 'Foreboding':

the future's about to leap at you
like a baboon with a hatchet
from a man-hole or a closet, screaming

That image, for me, sums up more eloquently than a review can do, what it is that makes Kevin Higgins really good. It's difficult, when so much has already been said, to avoid trotting out the old clichés: satirical, caustic, Larkin-esque. Yes, Higgins is all those, but what sometimes gets missed in all the discussion about content and tone, is the craft that underpins these poems. The images are surprising, infused with humour and accuracy. Each line is measured to Higgins' breath worked so the break occurs always on the strong word. The use of rhyme is usually subtle and backgrounded so that it seems almost accidental or incidental to the poem, but assonance, alliteration, and various types of half and off-rhyme are present none the less. Take for example the lines below from 'The Doctor's Waiting Room'

Your road rage face
strategic tears and apologies always
like artificial Los Angeles snow.
Hate him, breathless and red faced as ever.
You taking the world warmly by the throat.

Look closely and as well as assonances on 'snow' and 'throat', and 'breathless' and 'ever', 'face' and 'always', there are various alliterative groupings and echoes on Rs, Ts, Ws and Hs. Higgins is an accomplished performer of his work, a winner of several major slams, and this aspect of his work should not be understated when discussing his work. Indeed, the page

never tells all the story with Higgins and to make the poems really live, you have to hear Higgins deliver them.

Higgins takes us on a grand tour of his world in this book, there are elements of the bathetic in Higgins' wasteland, just as there are in Eliot's (and the title of the book is, I think, intended to point to the connection between them). Higgins ventriloquises several voices in this book, most of them acerbic; none of them repentant. He turns his invective against several targets, political and social in the main, with the Socialist movement being a favourite. Some of the poems address dysfunctional relationships, especially that favourite among Irish writers, the father – son problem. Yet Higgins is not afraid to poke fun at himself on occasion either as in 'This Small Obituary':

Your next-door neighbour will vaguely remember me,
when some hypocrite writes this small obituary:
"He had a real knack for last lines
but fell in love with his own invective
became such an expert at cutting throats
that, in the end, he slit his own."

Once or twice, the book could have done with a little tighter editorial eye, sometimes the same image recurs in too close proximity – for instance, clearly there is some fascination with three-bar fires, which occur in at least three poems, two of which are very close together. Perhaps they hold some symbolic association for Higgins, and are connected with the 'sad man in the caravan' who he says 'keeps coming back', but there appears to be a variety of association. The three-bar fire is used in symbolic nourishment where bread is toasted on it. It is next used as a symbol of run-down Bohemian chic, and thirdly as a way of describing sexual heat. Each image works in its own poem, but perhaps within the same book the repeated use is a little obtrusive.

That said, one tends to forgive Higgins his minor transgressions because the work is so joyously dark and funny. He is the only one of my Irish contemporaries who makes me laugh out loud regularly, not just because the work is funny, but because it has that great sense of character behind it, where one pictures the speaker in all his curmudgeonly grumpy-old-man-ness glaring at the reader wondering what the hell they're laughing at!

Nigel McLoughlin

Lost Republics
Alan Jude Moore
Salmon Poetry €12.00

Alan Jude Moore's second collection is split unequally into two sections. The first consists of poems dealing with his time in Russia and with a variety of aspects of life in capitalist Russia. He deals with feelings and ideas around estrangement, outsider-ness and belonging in the poems in that section. The second shorter section has poems set in Ireland, and Dublin particularly, followed by others, which range across Europe ending up, via Frankfurt and Antwerp, in Dubrovnik.

The structure of the book is interesting and one gets the feeling, reinforced by the cover design, that Moore has developed a certain sense of empathy with the people and culture of Russia through his time there, so much so that the movement across the second section feels like a movement home. The cover of the book has the author's name and the title shadowed in Cyrillic script and one feels that this is not accident or gimmick, but that part of Moore's identity demands that shadow sense of Russian-ness. Perhaps this is why the poems in the second section, even the Irish ones, have more of the sense of travelogue than the Russian based poems do. By that I mean that the Russian poems are more about the poet's internal state of being in Russia. They are not really concerned with describing what the poet sees as a tourist might, but what he feels about what he has observed and experienced. Paradoxically, some of the Dublin based poems have that concern for description of what is seen that one would

expect of the outsider.

The sunlight belongs to children
Dancing through cracks in the curtains
Hiding in gables and alcoves over Trinity
And all the tiny passers-by

Construction cranes draped in Christmas decorations
beg your attention
                                                    'Network'

Whereas in the poems in section one, the description lacks that need to make place explicit, and could really be set anywhere. They are sensitive to the predicament of post- communist Russia and are infused with loneliness, a downbeat sensibility and an almost elegiac quality. The poems are much more about the internal experience of being in the place:
Two years of service still to come.
Down on the border where the girls are crying.

The street is paved with petrol and tears
listing through the cracks of an old museum.
People wait on the steps for a faded pair of eyes,
A smile or expression to say goodbye to.

'Fine Art (at the Pushkin Museum)'

The poems in this book are well observed and well worked sets of images which are coupled to a keen ear for the music of language. The line is controlled very well indeed and Moore has the ability to handle the long line and the more staccato rhythm well in terms of their musical unities and with sensitivity as to how they operate as units of sense. He mixes and matches these adeptly as he deems necessary in many of the poems.

The dust of conversations
the history of affairs
dragged through the snow on the sole of a jackboot.
You left it there; the heart wandered to a different shore.
                                        'Zaped (West)'

Many of the poems in section one are dated at the bottom (one is actually dated in Russian) and one wonders what importance that has for the reader. I felt the dates distracted me, and I could not find any real significance to them, and although they may serve as aide-mémoires for the author, they could, and should, have been removed. This is more an editorial issue than a quality one. I would also be remiss if I did not point out what appears to be a misspelling of Agnus Dei in 'Route' where it is rendered as Agnes(sic) Dei.

Lost Republics will cement Moore's reputation as one of the better recently emerging Irish poets, one whose voice is distinctive, contemplative and able to draw on and create from the tradition of Mandlestam and Akhmatova, whose stylistic echoes can be seen in many of the poems, as well as the tradition of Austin Clarke and Derek Mahon whose influence I also detect.

Nigel McLoughlin

Listings

SUNDAY

Every Sunday
Welcome To Wormworld
Open mic, spoken word, performance
MC & DJ: Vis the Spoon
Free entry 8pm (open mic sign-in) at:
The Foundry,
84 Great Eastern Street,
Shoreditch.
Tel: 0207 736 6900

First Sunday of each month
Buzzwords.
Writing workshop, open mic, guest poet
7pm for the workshop, 8pm for readings £3 at
The Exmouth Arms,
Bath Road,
Cheltenham.
Tel 07855 308122
or email cheltpoetry@yahoo.co.uk

Third Sunday of every month.
PUREandGOODandRIGHT
Performance poetry,
The Fox,
32 Clarendon Avenue,
Leamington Spa,
CV32 4RZ.
7.30pm.
Admission £3 (£2 OAPS & NUS)
Open Mic slots available
http://www.kellywit.com/web/
pureandgoodandright.htm

First & Third Sunday of each month
Aromapoetry
Spoken word. Open mic. Free entry. Start
time to be determined.
New Venue: Charterhouse Bar, 38 Charter-
house Street, London EC1 Tel: 0207 608 0858
aroma@x-bout.com & www.x-bout.com

TUESDAY

Last Tuesday of every month
Poetry Open-Mic Night at Borders
Last Tuesday of Every Month
Free Entry 6.30 pm at Borders, 120 Charing
Cross Rd, London WC2H tel: 020 7379 8877

First Tuesday of each month,
Open Mic night,
The Tin Angel,
Medieval Spon
Street,
Coventry.
7.30pm start.
avocado_magazine@hotmail.com.
www.heaventreepress.co.uk.

Third Tuesday of the Month,
SHP Poets,
workshop from 7pm, performance
from 9pm, £2 entry.
South Hill Park,
Ringmead,
Bracknell
RG12 7PA

WEDNESDAY

Every Wednesday
**Express Excess: mix of comedy, poetry,
storytelling** at: The Enterprise, 2 Haverstock
Hill (chalk farm tube) Doors: 8.30, show 9pm
£5/£3 Tel: 020 7485 2659
www.expressexcess.co.uk

First Wednesday of Every Month
Big Mouth Cabaret
Marlows,
1 New Market Avenue,
Bristol
BS1 2EH

Doors 7.30 p.m. Show 8.00pm.
Tickets £6.00/£5.00 with flyer
Information: Rosemary Dun 0117 963 6462,
mobile 0777 154 6919

Every second Wednesday, 7.30pm, free.
Spoken Word
Drum Arts Centre, 144 Potters Lane, Aston
B6 4UUB. Contact RoiGriot@netscape.net

First Wednesday of each month
Dead Good Poets Society
Doors open 8pm, poetry starts at 8.30pm.
£1 Everyone welcome - each person has five
minutes to perform, and there are a maximum
of 24 slots delivered across three sets. Third
Wednesday of each month is Guest Night.
Everyman Bistro,
Hope Street,
Liverpool 1

Last Wednesday of every month
2 Many Poets
Spoken Word and Stand-up Poetry
£3 8pm (doors) 9pm (show) at the Pleasure
Unit Bar, 359 Bethnal Green Road, London E2
For more info contact Luke on 07973 440608
or info@2manypoets.com, 2manypoets.com

THURSDAY
Every Thursday
Shortfuse
Spoken word poetry
£5/ £3 8.30 pm (doors) at The Camden Head,
Camden Walk, Islington,
London, N1
www.20six.co.uk/shortfuse

First Thursday of every month
X-Press Delivery
A fusion of spoken word poetry and live music
£4/ £3 at Chez Manny Restaurant, 145-149
Battersea High Street, London SW11 tel:
07939 259 735,
Healution_inc@hotmail.com
First Thursday

Chapter Arts Centre
in Cardiff, organised by Seren Boooks on the
first Thursday of the month starting 8.00pm,
entry £2.00/£1.00concessions
Each event features readings by two guest
poets, followed by an open-mic spot, where
members of the audience will be invited to
perform their own work.
Information: willatkins@seren-books.com
seren-books.com
Tel: 01656 663018

Second Thursday of each month. 8pm. Free
Albert Poets
The Albert Hotel
(next to Huddersfield Library)
Victoria Lane,
Huddersfield,
HD1 2QF
Contact: albertpoets@live.co.uk

Last Thursday in the month 7:30pm at
**LibraAries Books, Mill Road
Cambridge.**
Open to published poets and beginners.
Contact geoffreywrites@yahoo.uk

Second Thursday of the month
Ambit:
Readers to be confirmed
£4/£3 6.30pm (doors)/7.30pm (start) at:
The Bath House Pub,
96 Dean Street,
Soho W1
tel: 0208 340 3566
or visit www.ambitmagazine.co.uk

Last Thursday of every month
Dylan Thomas Centre: Last Thursday
A night of readings and song with floor spots
for local writers.
£4/£2.80/£1,60 (Swansea PTL & floor per-
formers) 7.30 pm at:
The Dylan Thomas Centre,
Somerset Place,
Swansea SA1 1RR
Tel: 01792 463980,

WORKSHOPS & COURSES

La Rivolte
Runs poetry workshops each summer.
For more details contact Sarah on 020 7404
0984, e-mail larivolte@aol.com, visit www.
larivolte.com or write to Sarah Johnson,
Poetry Workshops, 83 Saffron Hill, London
EC1N 8RT

Poetry (and Prose) at the Abbey is
a series of 4 residential weekends run by
'Writers Inc.', brought to you by the Blue
Nose Poets, at an attractive 13th century
Abbey in Sutton Courtenay in Oxfordshire.
Variously using guest writers and the Blue
Nose poets' own expertise the weekends
involve writing exercises, tutorials and
readings as well as some space and peace to
write. The weekends start from only £99
residential and £89 non-residential.
Contact Blue Nose Poetry, P.O. Box 29695,
London E2 0FD Tel: 020 8981 2548 or email
Brettvt@btinternet.com.

Salmon Creative Writing Workshops
Salmon Publishing run regular weekend
creative writing workshops at the Salmon
premises: Knockeven, Cliffs of Moher, Co.
Clare. These include all aspects of writing
and publishing. The facilitator is Salmon's
director, Jessie Lendennie, who has conducted
workshops all over Ireland and the U.S., for
many years. Fee for the weekend is £100,
including B&B accommodation in the lively
village of Doolin.
Numbers are limited to 7 per weekend.
Sessions will run two weekends per month.
For more information, or to book, email
salpub@iol.ie or telephone 065 81941.
Salmon Publishing Website: http://www.
salmonpoetry.com/